Goat Crazy

How to Have the Healthiest, Best Producing, Longest Living Goats in the Land.

Pat James

Copyright Notice

This publication is designed to provide accurate and authoritative information in regard to the subject matter covered. It is sold the understanding that the publisher is not engaged in rendering legal, accounting, or other professional services. If legal advice or other expert assistance is required, the services of a competent professional person should be sought.

First Printing, 2012

ISBN-13: 978-1480256934

ISBN-10: 1480256935

Printed in the United States of America

No Liability

The information and resources in this book are not intended to be a substitute for professional advice. While all attempts have been made to verify the information provided

Table of Contents

Introduction

Goats are among the earliest of all known domesticated animals. Archeologists discovered the remains of goats in Asia, being able to date this animal back to 6000 and 7000 BC. History also shows us that goats, along with sheep, were hunted for food during the Old Stone Age with the use of traps.

Interestingly, goats have always been an important animal in Greece for dairy and meat. However, sometime around 7000 BC the number of people living in Greece grew substantially, making it more and more difficult to find food.

Thousands of years ago, goats were hunted primarily with the use of spears but over time as farming became an agricultural necessity, it was discovered that goats were also beneficial for other things such as milk and dairy products, hair, horns, and skin. Realizing the increased value of the goat, fenced pens and pastures were constructed as a means of keeping both goat and sheep protected from wild animals.

With goats being maintained in pens, people soon began to see that this animal was actually very friendly and docile, serving to increase the production of goat milk and dairy products. Although goats would one-day become valuable for hair, clothing, and textiles, during this time, this discovery had not yet been made, resulting in farmers using the wool from sheep and other animals.

Even the Bible teaches us that goats were tamed before the birth of Christ. In the 1400s when Greece was conquered by the Ottoman Empire and with the Islamic faith not permitting the consumption of pigs, goat meat became even more valuable. Today, goat is still a popular choice of meat for many regions around the world. For people with lactose intolerance, goat milk provides an excellent substitute. We also see goats now being used for their hair, for education in petting zoos, for breeding, and many other uses.

During the early days of exploration, it was common for sailors to keep goats on the vessels, which provided the men with a constant supply of meat and milk. The dairy goat migrated to North Africa and to the southern parts of Europe where over time, they were shipped to North America as a means of promising early settlers an ample supply of milk and cheese. Because of their versatility, goats have remained a very important part of a farmer's economy.

As you will discover in this book, goats come in a number of species that fall in the Bovidae family, which are ruminant, cloven-hoofed, and horned animals. Since goats have a stomach with four parts and chew their cud similar to that of a cow, they fall in the sub-order Ruminant. The female is called a "doe", "goat", or "nanny" and can be distinguished by her smaller horns. The male goat is known as a "buck" or "billy goat" that tends to be larger. Finally, the young goats are called "kids".

The animal tribe of Caprini is comprised of both goats and sheep since they are closely related. The primary difference is that a goat has a shorter tail and the horns are hollow, long, and pointed upward, backward, or even outward whereas a sheep will have horns that spiral. In addition, goats have beards while sheep do not. Although there are many similarities between goats and sheep, goats tend to be a little more curious, they have fun, inquisitive person-alities, and act more child like, making them great pets.

Domesticated goats have two unique traits that were passed down from their wild ancestors. First, they are extremely surefooted. Because of their stability, a wild goat is capable of climbing high into the mountains where they will stand almost vertically on small, narrow ledges. Even tame goats will use this natural talent for climbing on roofs or for getting into places that you would think impossible. This surefootedness is due in part to the design of the hooves.

The bottom of the hooves is similar to a suction cup while the inner layer called the subunguis, works as a shock absorber. This way, the goat can jump from rock to rock, sticking the landing while not damaging the foot from impact. To protect the hooves, keeping them strong and durable, the outer layer or unguis naturally wears down as needed. Second, goats eat just about anything, although not everything is good for them. For instance, it is common to see a goat eating grass, leaves, berries, cloth, dry wood, and other items.

Goats, whether domesticated or wild, have a very strong herding instinct. They love to play games and romp around together. Typically, a goat will breed during the fall months although some of the miniature breeds are capable of breeding throughout the year. The goat will remain pregnant for approximately 145 days at which time she will have two kids, although triplets are common.

Today, goats are raised domestically and again, are used as a common source of meat and milk. In addition, goats can produce thick hair for textiles and apparel, they are often used for pack animals, they can be skinned for leather, goats work in zoos or circuses, and some are simply kept as family pets. Although there are many excellent breeds, one that most people associate with is called the Kashmir goat, native to Kashmir, India and the producer of mohair. From this goat, the soft and expensive cashmere sweater is created.

This fun, alert, and inquisitive animal is truly enjoyable and beneficial. While we have touched on just a few aspects of the goat as a general overview, you can be sure there is much more to learn. This book will walk you through the various breeds, behavioral characteristics, eating habits, sleeping patterns, breeding, disease and illness, and much more.

We hope you enjoy this book and learn everything you need to know about goats! Thank you for buying Goat Crazy.

Further valuable goat information is available on our website at:

http://www.keeping-goats.com/

Understanding Goats

In this chapter, we will discuss the different behaviors, personalities, characteristics, social habits, and even languages associated with the goat. If considering buying a goat, you will quickly discover that each has its own specific behavior. While some goats share characteristics, others will display very individual behaviors.

Goat Language

Goats make a distinctive noise called "bleating." The interesting aspect of this sound is that much like humans or other animals, a goat will use variations of bleating as a means of sending different messages. As an example, when a goat greets a person or another goat, it will produce a light sounding bleat that almost sounds happy.

When a mother goat calls out to her young, the bleating takes on an almost desperate cry. This message is produced from the nose, which is very similar to a rattle meant as a warning for others to stay away. Anytime a goat is in pain, the bleating becomes a deep, groan-like sound. However, if the goat were ill, the bleating would likely be persistent.

As you raise goats and spend more time around them, you will soon become aware of the different sounds. Before long, you will be able to associate various tones with specific situations. Some people become so good at mimicking the sound, they can actually hold a conversation with their goat, although how intelligent is still to be determined.

Goat Nature

By nature, goats are very inquisitive and sometimes, nosey. They have an alert, curious sense about them, always eager to see what is happening. Because goats tend to be adventurous, they can sometimes find themselves in situations difficult to get out of, which is where their jumping and climbing abilities come in handy.

Therefore, if you head out to the barn to feed your goat and suddenly find it missing, do not panic. Instead, take a minute to check out the loft, under hay piles, or other unsuspecting places. Because goats are mischievous, they make fun and comical pets that are always willing to put on a show.

Social Habits

In most cases, goats are a sociable creature, preferring to be around people, goats, or other animals. Because they are more of a herd animal, you would probably have a happier goat if he or she has a companion. In the herd, goats have a definite pecking order by which the head doe and buck share the leadership role. Then, as new goats are brought into the herd, dueling will occur so a new ranking order can be established.

While this might appear scary to the goat owner, remember this is the goat's natural behavior. Therefore, allow the goats to work it out among themselves, which they will. Even when it seems brutal, very seldom does is a goat hurt. Now, if you want a pet, probably the best breed would be one of the miniature goats.

These breeds are similar to pet dogs in that they love to be brushed, walked, stroked, and talked to softly. The miniature goat is a highly intelligent animal that can be taught to perform tricks. In fact, the miniature goat can sometimes be housebroken. The various breeds of goats will be discussed in detail further in the book.

Characteristics of Goat Breeds

As you will discover in this chapter, there are a number of excellent goat breeds. The breed you choose will depend largely on the purpose for getting the goat. Obviously, if you want a goat for milking, you would need a good dairy goat. However, if you plan to keep the goat strictly for a family pet, you have quite a few choices.

In the United States alone, there are approximately 10 primary breeds of goats. Included are five dairy breeds, two meat breeds, two miniature or dwarf breeds, and then the Angora goat, which produces mohair. The information below can be used as a guide when choosing your goat, keeping in mind your specific needs. However, for additional information beyond what we have provided, we recommend you contact your local cooperative extension agent or the breed association for the specific breed interested in buying.

Keep in mind that for the sake of this book, we have included the ten breeds most commonly used in the United States, as well as a few other breeds commonly used in other countries. Just remember that you have multiple options so before buying, consider all the breeds that are best suited for your needs, regardless of the country of origin.

Dairy

All of the goats in this section are perfect for milking and many of them make great pets. Dairy goats are generally used for milk but some produce better milk and cheese than others do. You will find that goat cheese has a very deep, distinct flavor. Therefore, if you want a goat specifically for milk and cheese, you want to choose the best breed. The five breeds you see most often in the United States include Alpine, LaMancha, Nubian, Saanen, and Toggenburg.

Alpine

Alpine goats are also sold as French Alpine for the Alps from which this goat originates. Alpine goats are considered a medium to large breed with ears that point upward. In addition, this particular goat is very hardy, being able to adapt well to any environment. The Alpine goat is a seasonal breeder and available in several patterns and colors.

For milk rating, this breed receives 3.5% for butterfat. Because the milk production of the Alpine goat is so high when compared with other dairy goats, this breed is also called the "Holstein of goats". For example, a production of ten pounds or more of milk daily is considered quite common.

You will also hear the Alpine goat called the "French Alpine". For registration purposes, the papers include two designations, which are synonymous. This goat is considered a medium to large breed that is graceful, highly alert, and the only breed with upright ears. Additionally, because the Alpine goat comes in every imaginable color and color combination, it also has sub-names used to identify the various markings. Some of these include the following:

Broken

Broken Chamoisee/Chamoise – Meaning a solid Chamoisee or Chamoise that is broken with another color in the form of a splash or band

Chamoise/Chamoisee

Chamoisee (Female) and Chamoise (Male) – Meaning bay or brown, the markings are characterized as a black face, dorsal stripe, feet and legs, and on occasion, martingale running across the withers, down to the chest.

Cou Blanc

Cou Blanc – Meaning white neck, this color pattern consists of white front quarters and black hindquarters with gray or black markings on the goat's head

Cou Clair

Cou Clair – The translation means clear neck whereby the goat has tan, off-white, or saffron front quarters along with shading to gray with black on the hindquarters

Cou Noir

Cou Noir – This means black front quarters and white hindquarters

Pied

Pied – Meaning to have mottled or spotted markings

Sundgau

Sundgau – These markings are black with white, often seen on the underbody or as facial stripes

Two-Tone Chamoise/Chamoisee

Two-Tone Chamoisee/Chamoise – This refers to light colored front quarters and gray or brown hindquarters

LaMancha

This medium to large size breed is from Spanish origin although it was actually developed in the United States. When it comes to milking temperament, the LaMancha has one of the best. Considered extremely friendly and healthy, this seasonal breeder is a great, all-around choice for dairy.

The LaMancha goat also has small, elf-like ears that hook. Measuring just two inches or less, these ears are sometimes referred to as "gopher ears", which look like sweet rolls. The butterfat for the LaMancha is around 4.2%.

Nigerian Dwarf

This miniature goat comes from West Africa. The Nigerian Dwarf has pointed upright ears and although they are miniature in size, the breeding creates the appearance of proportion for length and structure to that of a standard dairy goat. This breed is available in several colors and patterns, and breeds throughout the year. While the butterfat percentage is 6.1%, due to small teats milking can be a challenge.

Nubian

Also called the Anglo Nubian, this goat is rather large yet graceful and proud. The ears are long and the nose Romanesque and distinguished. The creation of the Nubian goat was accomplished by breeding bucks of Indian and African origin with British goats. This breed is available in several colors and patterns, is a hardy, seasonal breeder, and tends to be vocal.

Although it does not generally produce large quantities of milk, the Nubian goat averages butterfat around 4.6%. For people wanting a gentile pet while taking advantage of moderate milk production for personal use, this is a popular choice of breed.

Oberhasli

This goat is also called a Swiss Alpine. The breed has a nice bay color with very distinctive, black markings. Keep in mind that although the Oberhasli comes in black, for some reason most people prefer the bay color. This goat is medium size, is a seasonal breeder, and produces milk with a butterfat of 3.6%.

Saanen

Originating in Switzerland, this is a large, white goat with upright ears. Although not common, the Saanen goat can be born with color. When this occurs, the name changes to

Sable. Even so, these are seasonal breeders and heavy milk producers with lower butterfat that averages 3.5%.

Toggenburg

This dairy goat is considered the oldest of all dairy breeds. The body is medium size and the ears stand upright. The coloring varies from a soft fawn to a rich chocolate, both with notable white markings. This seasonal breeder was originally used for the production of cheese since milk can be a bit overpowering. Even so, some people prefer the powerful flavor of the 3.3% butterfat.

Meat

Just as some people buy goats specifically for milk or pets, other people purchase goats for the meat. Although goat meat is more popular in other countries, it is becoming more popular in the United States as people are becoming aware of its many benefits. The primary breed used for the production of meat is the Boer goat, which comes from New Zealand and South Africa.

Boer

The Dutch word, "Boer" means farmer. First developed in South Africa, Boer goats have a Roman nose and long ears. Most of the goats have a white body with dark patterns around the head. The horns of this breed curve backwards, making it easy to distinguish. Although the Boer goat is strong and energetic, it is also a very gentle breed. This year round breeder is considered a favorite for the meat that is flavorful and tender.

The challenging aspect of buying a Boer goat is that telling a full-blooded one from a mixed breed is difficult. Although there seems to be some controversy surrounding the pedigree of this goat, most experts agree that the full-blooded Boers come from South Africa. Not only is this the expert's opinion but it appears to be a well-documented fact.

Therefore, if you want to ensure you buy a Boer goat that is full-blooded, it must be South African regardless of color or color combination. Known also as the "Spanish" goat, it is estimated that the Boer goat first came from Spain sometime in the 1500s. Although raised mostly for the meat, this particular breed also produces a significant amount of soft cashmere.

In the western United States, the Boer goat is used by ranchers wanting to clear out weeds and brush from their pastures. This practice has continued through the years where today, you can find a number of programs whereby the Boer goat is used for clearing land that would be too costly with modernized means.

Kiko

Kiko translates to "meat" or "flesh". This breed came from feral goats out of New Zealand that are best known for their ability to survive in harsh conditions. The Kiko goat is a good breeder that will produce kids throughout the year.

Spanish

The Spanish goat is also referred to as the "Brush" goat. This breed was brought to North America by European explorers. The body size is medium although somewhat muscular and stocky. The Spanish goat comes in several colors. Considered a hardy breed, this goat produces kids all year long.

Tennessee Fainting

If you have never seen a Tennessee Fainting goat in action, no words could be used to explain the phenomena from which they got their name. Also known as "Nervous", "Myotonic", Stiff-legged", "Wooden Leg", "Tennessee Meat", and "Scare", this breed ranges in size from small to medium.

Without doubt, the Tennessee Fainting goat is extremely, unique. Its behavior called "Myotonia Congenital" causes the muscles to lock up whenever the goat becomes startled or scared. When this occurs, the goat will literally fall over where it stands. Then, it will lie down completely stiff legged.

The Tennessee Fainting goat is available in several colors that include white, tan, brown, red, and black that comes in both long and short coats. In addition, these goats have one of three types of ears. The first is called "airplane" ears, which are long, angling toward the eyes, the second are short ears, and the third have a crimp along the end. Regardless, to be a true Tennessee Fainting goat, the ears must be creased.

Miniature

The goats listed in this section are very small. Because of this, the miniature breeds are often kept as pets much like the potbelly pig. Different from standard goats, the miniature breeds come from the Caprine family as ruminants, meaning they are cud-chewing creatures that have a four-chambered stomach.

Miniature breeds will produce kids twice annually and in fact, it is common for them to have twins and even triplets. After being weaned from the mother's milk around two months of age, the goat will go on to live a long, healthy life, many times reaching 15 years or older.

African Pygmy

The Pygmy goat comes from Africa and as the name suggests, the breed is very small. Interestingly, the Pygmy is considered a meat goat, especially in its natural origin. However, today you find this breed purchased and kept as pets primarily because of its cute, small size.

This particular goat is heavy boned and available in many different colors with unique markings. The Pygmy is very low maintenance, measuring 22 inches tall or less although the average size is 16 inches. In addition, the Pygmy goat weighs on average just 35 pounds.

Nigerian

The Nigerian Dwarf goat comes from the west central portion of Africa. This breed of miniature goat is considered an excellent milk producer, being capable of making up to two quarts daily. Typically, this goat measures 22 inches tall or less, averages 16 inches tall, and similar to the Pygmy goat, weighs on average 35 pounds. Bred to produce several colors, the Nigerian goat is known for its beautiful blue eyes.

Miscellaneous

Other goats are used for a number of purposes – perhaps a family pet, as a pack animal, entertainment, and so on. Typically, the goats in this section would be used in these ways.

Angora

This type of goat is known for its extremely long hair, also called mohair. Being of Turkish origin, the Angora is medium in size and a seasonal breeder. Although considered a very hard breed, the Angora is also docile and laid back.

Kinder

This breed of goat is listed in the "miscellaneous" category simply because it is actually a dual breed. Considered both a meat and dairy goat, the Kinder was developed in the United States by cross breeding a Nubian with a Pygmy. The kinder is a nice breed that comes in many different colors and patterns.

Pygora

This particular breed of goat came about by a woman named Katherine Jorgensen. In breeding the Pygora, she wanted a goat that would produce fine fiber that could be used best for hand spinning. To accomplish this, she took an Angora and Pygmy with the result being exactly what she expected. The Pygora goat produces the most amazing hair – soft and silky.

Scrub

The term "scrub" is actually a catchall phrase for mutts or goats that have mixed breeding or those that are an unknown breed.

Horned Goats

When it comes to horned sheep and goats, many people get them confused. Take the horned sheep for example. The Barbados Black Belly breed is known for its distinct markings.

For a sheep to be deemed a Barbados Black Belly, strict guidelines on color must be followed, which include the belly and inside of the legs being black. In addition, the sheep must have two black bars running down the front of the face, just on the inside of the eyebrows, and then going down to the muzzle.

The Barbados Black Belly sheep would also have to have some black wrap around the legs, black in the front from the knees down on the front legs, a black line across the top of the head, dark brown, red, or tan coloring on the back and sides, and black on the pointed ears and chin.

Then, for a ram, you would see heavy hair on the neck along with a long, heavy mane. Finally, most of these sheep have some level of black or a heavy black line on the underside of the neck. The key difference is that sheep have fleece while goats have hair.

Other differences are that sheep do not have horns, only goats. In addition, goats are actually much smarter than sheep, they do not gorge themselves like sheep, they browse while sheep graze, and finally, goats are generally not very timid around people whereas sheep are very skittish.

Common Types of Illness and Injury

Goats, just like any other animal, do become ill or suffer from injury. This chapter will focus on common ailments associated with goats, as well as recommended solutions. Obviously, whether the goat will be used for meat, dairy, or merely kept as a family pet, it is imperative that the goat be in top health.

Agalactia

This infectious disease occurs when milk is not secreted in the mother goat's breast after her kid has been delivered. With Agalactia, there are typically three distinct symptoms, which include articular, mammary, and ocular. With Agalactia, either the entire herd of goats is affected with serious forms of manifestations, or sporadic clinical cases are followed by quiet periods.

The problem with Agalactia is that there will be a carrier among the goats, keeping the disorder running rampant. With goats, the more serious concern would be on the auricular mycoplasma, which typically how Agalactia is introduced. With this, the disease is transmitted to a newborn kid through the mother's colostrums or milk. However, remember that milk is not the only culprit. In fact, any type of body secretion such as urine, feces, mucus, and so on could be the problem.

If the goat were infected with Agalactia, you would notice a significant reduction of milk production. In addition, the infected animal would show signs of eye and auditory infection. If the Agalactia is chronic, the only presentation may be the reduction in milk production, as well as atrophy involving the mammary glands. Although not always the case, respiratory problems can also develop with Agalactia.

Although some people will try antibiotic treatment, this solution is not often effective since there appears to be too much resistance. In fact, using antibiotics can often make the condition worse. Therefore, they should be avoided. Instead, using macrolides and quinolones is an excellent method of treatment for the infected goat. Keep in mind that the number one treatment option is to ensure you have proper control over any animals being introduced to a herd. In other words, being proactive is better than being reactive.

Beta Mannosidosis

This genetic defect is caused by a recessive gene that only affects Nubian goats. The only way to identify this defect is through DNA testing. Sadly, Beta Mannosidosis takes over quickly and is fatal. Interestingly, affected goats do not.grow up to breed and pass the gene along. Because of that, the number of incidences is less than 1%, with just 13% being potential carriers.

If a goat were born with the defect, you would notice symptoms very similar to the human disease, cerebral palsy. The goat would have difficulty standing, walking, holding its head up, and would shake uncontrollably. While it would be a challenge for the kid to suckle, once it can latch onto its mother's teat, it tends to calm down quickly. Other common problems associated with Beta Mannosidosis include skeletal deformities, the goat could be deaf, and it might have twitching eyes.

Beta Mannosidosis is caused when a certain enzyme that removes specific sugars from the cells is lacking. With this missing enzyme, sugar accumulates in the cells of the nervous system. As the level of sugar increases, the symptoms become far more noticeable, usually within a few weeks. Sadly, the condition will only worsen until eventually the kid will die.

CLA

Officially called Caseous Lymphadenitis, this disease is devastating among goats. CLA is a bacterium known as Corynebacterium pseudotuberculosis, responsible for causing two forms of infection. The first is superficial, which involves lymph nodes located just beneath the skin.

With this, you would notice one or more abscesses, typically around the neck, head, or body and/or leg junction. Over time, these abscesses will rupture and then drain. The second form of CLA is visceral, which not only involves the lymph nodes but also major organs of the body, particularly the liver and kidney.

Once a goat has CLA, it will begin to gain weight, which actually causes poor production of milk and a decreased value of the pricey pelt. The superficial form of this disease is bad enough but the second, internal form is ranked as the third most important cause of condemnation for carcasses in the United States. Even worse, CLA is a lifelong problem that runs its course of infection even when the goat appears healthy and normal.

The good news is that goats usually have the superficial form more than they do the visceral form. While both forms can affect both adult and young goats, you typically see the younger goats becoming infected easier. To date, there are no known cases of humans being infected with CLA in the United States but even so, warnings do go out regarding slight risk.

In other countries where human infection has been reported, the cause has been directly associated with people who hand skin goat carcasses. Generally, the individual has been cut with the knife used for skinning and thereby the infection is passed along. While humans in the United States have been safe thus far, it is imperative that any carcass handlers take great caution.

If you have goats infected with CLA, you will need to start by isolating infected goats from the healthy goats. Then, the area where the infected animals had been to include housing, feeders, fenced off pasture, and so on, will need to be properly disinfected. To minimize the risk of goats getting CLA, it is important to administer a toxoid vaccine once a year. In addition, always make sure the goats are not houses in crowded spaces.

Colds

Yes, goats struggle with the common cold just as humans do. Typically, you would notice a runny nose, cough, no temperature, and a slight level of lethargy. Some people will give their goat antibiotics every time they come down with a cold. Although you want to ensure the cold does not progress into something more serious such as pneumonia, generally a goat will fight the cold off naturally without the use of antibiotics.

To help your goat through a cold, provide dry bedding in a draft free and well-ventilated stall. In addition, oils such as eucalyptus, lavender, tea tree, and thyme can be placed in a humidifier. This type of aromatherapy is actually very beneficial. If you notice changes such as clear snot turning green, the lungs sounding raspy, and the goat running a temperature of more than 103.5 degrees, antibiotics should probably be given.

If the goat were not with kid, something like oxytetracycline would work quite well. On the other hand, if the goat is pregnant, then you could go with penicillin procaine or penicillin benzathine. It is important to keep stress levels down while battling the cold. To accomplish this, administer probios and use the scents of aromatherapy.

Finally, if a cough develops, pay attention since this could be associated with a cold or it could be a sign of Lungworm. If you notice heavy coughing after play but no other signs of trouble, your best bet would be to use a dewormer such as Lvomec.

Floppy Kid Syndrome

The Floppy Kid Syndrome is associated with metabolic acidoisis, known for causing serious weakness. The good news about this condition is that there is no organ involvement. However, both respiratory and gastrointestinal symptoms develop that include dyspnea, diarrhea, and dehydration. While veterinarians are aware of this condition, the full extent of the problem is not yet understood. For this reason, researchers are underway conducting more testing.

An affected kid will appear to be perfectly normal at birth but within three to ten days, it begins to show signs of muscle weakness. Many times, although the kid is hungry, it will have difficulty suckling. Both depression and marked paradoxical metabolic acidosis are also common symptoms. Once Floppy Kid Syndrome is suspected, additional testing will be performed. A firm diagnosis will usually show lower levels of bicarbonate, an increase in anion gap, and often an increased level of chloride.

To determine the severity of the Floppy Kid Syndrome, blood work is required. Because of the inability to suckle, kids often suffer from dehydration followed by diarrhea and slow breathing patterns. The degree in which care is provided is highly dependent on early detection and treatment options. For mild cases, the kid would be treated with oral bicarbonate. In addition, if the kid were having trouble suckling or were hesitant to suckle, it may need to be fed with a stomach tube.

If the kid has a more severe case of Floppy Kid Syndrome, usually an isotonic intravenous 1.3% sodium bicarbonate solution would be required. Once intravenous fluids are administered, the goat will generally come back very quickly. From there, the goat would need to be watched to ensure further treatment were not required. If a relapse were to occur, you would usually see it sometime between four and six weeks after treatment.

Foot Rot

Foot Rot is caused when there are improper levels of sulfur and copper in a goat's diet. This first begins as Foot Scald, which then worsens until it progresses into Foot Rot. While Foot Scald does not produce any type of foul odor, Foot Rot is very foul smelling. In fact, it is common to see a pussy discharge from the hoof area. This condition is serious and should be treated immediately.

The most common form of treatment for Foot Rot is to trim back the rotten part of the goat's hoof, which should be done by a trained veterinarian to ensure healthy tissue is not cut as well. Then, the infected area of the hoof should be scrubbed with a copper wash that includes two tablespoons of copper sulfate coupled with one-tablespoon vinegar mixed into one quart of water. Finally, any scabs or lesions would be sprinkled with copper sulfate powder, covered with clean dressing, and left for a minimum of 24 hours.

In addition to this treatment, a second solution should be prepared. This time, mix one-half teaspoon copper sulfate, one-teaspoon dolomite, and two teaspoons of vitamin C powder. This mixture should be given orally to the goat for two days. After the two days, the goat should be fed oats containing an adequate amount of sulfur and copper.

Once these treatments have been administered and the goats feed adjusted, the case of Foot Rot should clear up. If the Foot Rot is severe, your veterinarian may recommend antibiotics such as penicillin, streptomycin, or tetracycline with or without the mentioned treatments.

Foot Scald

Just above a goat's hooves is a line of hair. With Foot Scald, this hair would change or begin to fall out completely. This condition is caused by bacterium that is often found in consistently wet stalls or pastures. In addition, if the level of manure is high, this only contributes to the problem.

Foot Scald is a very serious condition that if not treated can cause marked lameness that develops fast. In fact, the problem can become so severe that the goat will struggle to stand. Many times other symptoms develop to include the skin located between the toes becoming painfully red and swollen or white and blanched. Either way this condition is extremely painful to the goat, which is why immediate attention is required.

Since Foot Scald and Foot Rot can go hand-in-hand, it is important to identify any problems and seek immediate care. Remember, if the problem were Foot Rot, you would not notice a foul odor whereas with Foot Rot, the smell is strong. In most cases, once you move the goat to a dry stall or pasture, the problem will clear up on its own. However, if the case of Foot Scald were severe, the affected foot would need to be bathed in 10% zinc sulfate.

Founder

Also called Laminitis, this problem shows up quickly as lameness. Once a goat has a problem with Founder, you would actually notice a hot or cold sensation when touching the feet. Founder is caused by low levels of magnesium or a sudden consumption of high protein, which would come from a recent change of diet or raids on feed bins.

To treat Founder, the goat should be fed a special mixture consisting of two tablespoons Epsom salts. In addition, you would find it beneficial to add dolomite to the feed. As the magnesium level begins to stabilize, the Founder will clear up without further treatment.

G-6-S

This genetic defect affects dairy goats, as well as other types of animals. Officially called Mucopolysaccharidosis IIID, it is estimated that approximately 25% of all Nubian goats have this gene with just about all of them being carriers.

Typically, if the defect exists the goat would not grow. Although the affected kid usually appears smaller than a healthy kid does, this is not always the case. In fact, some people have reported that their affected kid grew perfectly normal for two to three months and then suddenly stopped growing.

Goats with this gene lack substantial muscle mass, have block-shaped heads, live with a compromised immune system, and may be blind or deaf, or both. Usually, the goat will die a young age from heart failure although there have been instances when goats lived until the age of three or four. The problem with G-6-S is that the symptoms can be associated with other problems as well. Therefore, proper diagnosis is imperative.

The only option for correcting the problem is by removing the gene defect, which would require extensive DNA testing. The interesting aspect of this defect is that even humans have the same gene known as Sanfilippo IIID. Even children with this defect would appear as normal growing children until suddenly, they stop growing.

Just as with the goats, affected humans suffer from muscle loss, have neurological deterioration, and eventually die. The only good news, if you can call it that, is with humans also suffering from the same defected gene, studies are underway to find a cure. Once a cure for humans has been identified, it is expected that goats too would benefit from the same treatment.

Lice

Goats get lice just as people do. Some people think their goat has fleas but according to veterinarians, goats do not get fleas. To correct the problem with lice, you can use CoRal powder, which is a great solution. If lice were on a kid, you would need to adjust the amount of powder used not to cause harm.

Listeriosis

Listeriosis is a type of bacterial infection that most often affects the goat's brain. Considered common, the signs associated with this disease include spontaneous abortion and disorders associated with the central nervous system. The bacterium that causes Listeriosis is called Listeria Moncytogenes, which lives in the ground, grass, and manure. Interestingly, if the pH level in soil is 5.4 or higher, Listeria thrives.

If you have goats, it is crucial that any silage be compact for proper fermentation. Listeriosis is also found in moist hay bales so always make sure feed is kept completely dry. While cattle and sheep have low resistance to this disease, goats are exceptionally resistant. Even so, goats can be infected with Listeriosis, showing signs that include loss of appetite, depression, and fever.

Sometimes, another illness known as "circling disease" can occur with Listeriosis. With this, the goat literally begins to walk around in circles. Other common symptoms include a lack of coordination, rubbing or leaning against objects, and eventually, paralysis. Once symptoms first appear, the goat will die within three to four days. If the goat is pregnant, she will usually abort around 12 weeks.

The most important aspect in treating this disease is recognizing it. Usually, a good broad-spectrum antibiotic will make a remarkable difference. Although vaccines are not available in all countries, they are available in the United States. The problem with Listeriosis is that humans who have low immune systems can also be affected. For this reason, if you work around a goat that shows signs of this disease, you should also be tested.

Mastitis

Mastitis is inflammation of the mammary glands, often the cause of bacteria. If you have a goat with this condition, first ensure she is eating and being given lots of love and support. Many times, the new mother will lose her appetite, which is common. However, if she stops eating, the condition will quickly take her downhill.

To help get your goat back on track, penicillin shots twice daily for five to seven days should be administered. If the Mastitis is severe, the treatment period of antibiotics may need to be extended. Keep in mind that if the Mastitis appears before five days of giving birth, there is some risk of milk fever from intensive milking, which is a common cure for Mastitis. On the other hand, if the Mastitis appears right after birth, the kids are not suckling enough milk.

Remember, if the doe is not producing adequate milk, she is at risk for Mastitis. However, if she has a large udder and appears to be producing significant milk risk of Mastitis could also exist. In other words, this condition can manifest in a number of ways. Therefore, as a rule of thumb, express one-fifth of the doe's milk per day. In other words, if the doe delivered three days prior and Mastitis appears, you want to express three-fifths of her milk.

If the doe delivered five or more days prior, go through the normal milking process. Then, rub the teats followed by milking, repeating the process for 10 to 15 minutes. When done, very gently inject 2ml penicillin into each of her teats. If you are able to empty the udder without causing milk fever, the best solution for Mastitis is again, milking followed by rubbing the teats for 10 to 15 minutes.

If the udder is hot to the touch, apply ice packs to sooth her aching body. If the kids are nursing, the ice pack will also help make the teats softer and less painful for nursing. Remember that every case of Mastitis is different. Therefore, you will need to watch your goat to see how she responds, providing her with the appropriate treatment. If all else fails, talk to your veterinarian about additional solutions.

Parasites

One of the most common problems people face when raising goats is the battle against parasites, especially in the
south central and southeast portions of the United States.
Of all parasites, the worm is the worst. While there have
been a number of excellent treatment options developed
over the years, the challenge is that parasites are smart.

Once treated with a certain drug, the parasites become
highly resistant, meaning that drug no longer works. Because of this, you will need to stay on top of the parasite
problem by staying educated about new dewormer products on the market.

Barber Pole Worm

The   biggest   culprit   is   called   gastronintestinal
trichostrongyles, which is an entire family of worms. Of
these, the Barber Pole worm which can be fatal to goats.
The problem is that the worm attacks the goat by sucking
its blood, which in turn causes anemia. If you suspect your
goat has been infected with the Barber Pole worm, you
would most often notice paleness to the eye membranes.

The most effective form of parasite control appears to
include anthelmintics, which are dewormers. The problem
with worms is monumental. For that reason, as a goat
owner it is crucial to understand parasites, learning the
many ways in which they attack.

Adult female worms produce the eggs, which are then
passed in manure. These eggs hatch into larvae that go

through a number of developmental phases within the environment prior to infecting the next host. When theweather is warm, massive numbers of larvae build up in the pasture where your goats eat and live.

Interestingly, for the worms to be successful in the development process, they too need grass. In addition, the success of the larvae development relies on the climate with both warmth and moisture being crucial for survival. What happens is that the Barber Pole larvae get inside the goat's stomach via grass. There, the larvae will lie dormant, not turning into adult worms for months.

Armed with this knowledge, you can take the appropriate steps to control the huge army of parasites to keep your goats healthy. Remember that worms and goats usually go hand-in-hand so you always want to be prepared to control the situation. Remember that worms are especially resistant to treatment. Therefore, in addition to staying on top of new products to treat worms, you also want to use a few other techniques.

Tips to follow for prevention and treatment of worms and other parasites include:

Taking time to check your goats for anemia which would be seen as pale mucous membranes, especially around the eyes.

Allowing the goats to graze on pastures comprised of other types of vegetation than just grass. Since Barber Pole worms need grass to live, your goats should be offered other things to eat.

Making sure your goats are not kept in crowded conditions. Instead, they should have pastures to roam.

Feeding your goats only quality feed. In addition to providing the goats proper vitamins and minerals, a healthy diet will promote overall health.

Making sure kids are offered a full grazing season to help build up a natural immunity to parasites.

Being careful with drugs used for parasite control, choosing dewormers that are known to work while not causing any harm to the animal. In addition, use the right dosage and administer the drugs correctly. To reduce the possibility of drug resistance, rotate dewormers. Finally, check with the drug manufacturer to ensure you are using the right combinations for the safety of the goat and effectiveness.

Coccidia

Another common parasite seen with goats is called Coccidia. All goats have this internal parasite, which is perfectly normal. However, this parasite must be controlled so that it does not progress into a disease known as Coccidia.

These single celled protozoan organisms multiply within the host goat. From there, they produce oocysts, which are found in the goat's feces. With this, the environment is contaminated, which in turn infects other goats within a matter of days. The challenge with Coccidia is that oocysts are survivors, being capable of surviving up to one year.

Since they can live in barns, stalls, pastures, or any place where goat feces exists, the problem is ongoing.

Typically, kids are the goats infected although you will occasionally see an older goat with Coccidia, especially in dairy goats. Once infected, symptoms of a problem would include weight loss, low appetite, scours, and poor quality coat. If the Coccidia were severe, the goat could die quickly.

The best form of treatment for Coccidia is prevention although some treatments are successful. Start by keeping the goat's living area clean and sanitized. Then, use feed troughs that can be placed off the floor to ensure the goats are not eating off the ground. In addition, stalls should have excellent drainage and be kept completely dry. Finally, keep stables clean from manure.

Enteric Colibacillosis

With this disease, the goat would develop diarrhea, suffer from water, potassium, sodium, chloride, and bicarbonate loss, and develop metabolic acidosis. The kid would be affected within the first week of life at which time it would become weak, anorectic, and depressed. In this case, the goat would either get better or die, typically within five to seven days.

Kids at the greatest risk are those that do not ingest enough colostrum from the mother's milk. Other factors leading to this disease include crowded, cold, and dirty environments that make perfect breeding grounds for pathogens. Caused by strains of E. coli that attach to the small intestine, this disease is very harmful for baby goats.

The best treatment for Enteric Colibacillosis is fluid replacement for dehydration caused by diarrhea. Depending on the level of dehydration, the fluid treatment would be administered via IV or orally. Keep in mind that water should be alternated with an electrolyte solution and healthy goat's milk. The key here is not to mix the electrolytes with the milk in that this could cause casein clot.

Maedi-Visna / Caprine Arthritis Encephalitis

Both of these viruses are both persistent and progressive. Sadly, the virus will run its course very slowly, ending with multiple organ involvement and degeneration followed by cachexia and eventually death.

Typically, these viruses affect newborn kids of infected mothers. However, on rare occasion, the goat will go a lifetime being infected and never develop any of the lesions associated with the viruses. In most cases, the lungs, joints, nervous structures, and glands are affected. Depending on the case, the goat may have just one organ affected or several.

At first there would be delayed growth in the kid, weight loss and slowed walking or gait. As the disease progresses, things take a bad turn. If the viruses attack the respiratory system, the goat would experience cachexia or dyspnea.

If the mammary is affected, the bilateral mammary would harden. For the neurological form of the disease, paralysis is common. Finally, once the articular is affected, lameness develops. In addition to all this, the goat will begin to develop lesions that may or may not rupture.

To fight against these viruses, goats must have proper ventilation. Additionally, healthy herds must be produced from non-infected young goats and serological follow up should be performed. Once any seropositive goats are identified, they would be destroyed. If a kid is born to an infected mother, it should be moved to a clean area immediately after birth where for the first two days, it would be fed only healthy colostrums.

Meningeal Worm

Also called the "brain worm", the problem with this parasite is that it shows up without warning. Not only is this parasite hard to prevent but it is also a challenge to treat. Even so, some things can be done in the battle against the Meningeal worm.

Remember that the parasite's larvae are passed in the manure. The goat is infected by eating the grass or by consuming slugs and snails that have been snacking on the larvae. From there, the worm makes its ways to the goat's GI tract, traveling to the spinal cord via abdomen.

Along the pathway inside the goat, lesions will develop. Interestingly, some goats will have the Meningeal worm but show no symptoms at all while other goats will develop lameness. If the goat is severely infected, rear limb paralysis is often seen although the forelimbs can also be affected.

To treat an infected goat, an anthelminitic treatment is required. Unfortunately, even with treatment not all goats recover. To encourage success, it is highly recommended that an anti-inflammatory be administered and that the goat be fed only the highest quality food. Water should be completely replaced daily so it too is always fresh and clean. Obviously, eliminating this parasite is best done with prevention.

Young Ruminant Diarrhea

This problem is quite common in young goats, especially during the first two months of life. The goat will experience varying levels of diarrhea, which is caused by a pathologic agent such as salmonella, giardia, cryptosporidium, or a number of factors.

To combat this problem, simply take care to provide the goats with clean, dry bedding. In addition, be sure all manure and fecal matter is cleaned up from the floor, that food and water is raised off the floor, and that stalls are dry with adequate ventilation.

Septicemic Colibacillosis

This disease usually occurs during the first two weeks of a kid's life. The first symptoms include lethargy, depression, and then a watery type of diarrhea.

Other signs that might follow include abnormal mucus membrane, fever, and hypothermia. To treat this disease, expect to pay significant money and invest a lot of time. Due to the investment and potential risks associated with treatment, many people will have the goat humanly euthanized.

Dewormers

As mentioned, dewormers are tricky in that parasites become very resistant to their effectiveness. Because of this, new dewormers are being developed all the time.

The dewormers available today that are still successful in treating various parasites include those listed in this section. The challenge for goats is that as a worm becomes resistant to one drug within a family of drugs, it will be resistant to all the drugs in that same family. As you can imagine, this makes treatment difficult.

Benzimidazoles

Benzimidazoles – Goats are capable of metabolizing this drug much differently than sheep and therefore, must be given a higher dose. The family drugs include Albendazole, Fenbendazole, Oxfendazole, and Thiabendazole.

Levamisole

Levamisole – This dewormer is widely used in goats but again, goats need a much higher dose than sheep do. This particular product is a little riskier than other drugs, producing side effects such as salivation, specifically when administered the drug via shot. Although oral medication seems to produce fewer side effects, it also passes through the goat faster, meaning it may not be as effective as injections.

Lyermctin

Lyermctin – This drug is available in injectable form although for goats, the oral form seems to be more effective for some reason. In addition, milk withdrawal time is less when given as oral medication.

Morantel

Morantel – This product has many of the same characteristics as Pyrantel, which is an active ingredient found in a horse dewormer called Strongid. Although the drug is made for cattle, it has been shown effective with goats and has no milk withdrawal time.

For any dewormer to be effective with goats, the animal's weight must be calculated exact. If an under dose is given, the parasite will simply become resistant quickly. For this reason, experts recommend a dose 1.5 times the prescribed dose for goats. The recommendation is also to rotate dewormers every year for higher effectiveness rates.

The time required between dewormer treatment and milking the goat is another important consideration. With this, you must wait for the medication to pass through the goat before milk can be sold or consumed. The amount of time that passes depends on the type of drug, as well as dose given.

In general, the milk holding time in the United States is set at 36 days and in the United Kingdom, just 14 days. However, if you were to ask goat farmers in the United States what they do, most of the top producers would tell you they hold the milk just four to ten days! Remember, the 36 and 14 days respectively are guidelines.

The reason for the shorter withdrawal time depends on the drug used. For instance, with Lvomec, this drug is also used on humans in third-world countries. For that reason, it is believed that administering it to goats does not create any risk. When looking at the various dewormers, remember that the withdrawal time on the package is for cattle only, not on goats.

Another consideration is how much the goat is milked; meaning if the goat is milked for one or two people, the withdrawal time might need to be a little longer whereas if the goat were milked for ten people, the drug would be expressed out of the goat's system much faster.

Pinkeye

In goats, Moraxella Bovis is the most common cause of conjunctivitis, or pinkeye. The frustrating aspect of pinkeye is that there is no known cure. Therefore, the battle focuses more on controlling secondary infections, allowing the pinkeye to run its course.

With pinkeye, you may or may not notice a white, milky discharge from the eyes. As with other illnesses, the best option is to be proactive instead of reactive. The solution, vaccinating the goat at the start of the summer to help stop the problem before it begins. Remember that pinkeye in cattle is not the same as what you see with goats so it must be treated accordingly.

Although some people believe pinkeye is best caught in the early stages by using Tetracycline on the entire herd of goats, the truth is spending time and money treating each goat with antibiotics is simply a waste. Remember, that pinkeye is just one of those things that happen among cattle and goats. Therefore, allow the Pinkeye to run its natural course while treating the risk of potential infection.

One problem is that flies commonly transport the Pinkeye infection from one animal to another, which is why if one goat has this disease, they should all be treated, especially those that have been in close contact with the affected animal. Again, antibiotics are a good treatment option but more risk of secondary infection. In addition to antibiotics, you might consider trying any of the following medical and home remedies.

Furox

Branded under the name Furazolidine, this yellow spray-on powder has proven to be very successful for the treatment of Pinkeye. In addition to spraying in the eye twice daily, the entire area around the eye would also need to be treated. Using Furox typically clears the infection up in five to seven days.

Gentocin Pinkeye Spray

This spray is used for about one week, administered twice daily. This medication contains Gentamicin sulfate, which is a preferred treatment for many people that own goats. The nice thing about using this spray is that all of the ingredients can be purchased and the solution made at home.

Neopredef

If you know for sure the goat has Pinkeye, Neopredef powder is also a good treatment option that should be administered twice daily in both eyes. Neopredef contains both a
painkiller and antibiotic, meaning the goat receives pain
relief from the Pinkeye while the antibiotics fight off infection. With Neopredef, you would expect to see the Pinkeye
clearing up in about one week.

Oxybiotic

Branded under the name of Butler, this antibiotic is a great
treatment for Pinkeye, generally administered between the
goat's shoulder blades. The problem with this medication is
that it is painful when injected, making it an uncomfortable
treatment for the goat.

Oxytetracycline

Another great antibiotic for battling Pinkeye is
Oxytetracycline, branded under LA200. This particular
medicine is available in both eye drops and shot form. The
injection is painful for the goats, which is why most professional breeders highly recommend the drops, which goats
seem to handle much better.

Terramycin

Typically, using Terramycin is an excellent solution whenever Pinkeye moves into a secondary infection. This antibiotic is strong and great for controlling any secondary
infection.

Tetracycline

A number of options fall under the "tetracycline" category. However, two that many goat owners prefer are called Biomycin and ID-1, which is a relatively new product on the market. Both of these medications work extremely well in treating Pinkeye, as well as secondary infections.

Vinegar/Port Wine and Water

Home remedies for treating Pinkeye are also very beneficial. For example, one such remedy involves filling a spray bottle with equal amounts of vinegar or port wine and water. Shaken to mix well, the solution is then sprayed directly into the eye once daily.

Polio-Polioencephalomalacia

This problem is associated with a thiamin deficiency that is most common in ruminants. If the goat were infected, the symptoms would present as the goat wandering about, appearing disorientated, retracting the head, and in severe cases, the goat would go blind.

Other possible symptoms would include poor appetite, general weakness, and anorexia. With Polio-Polioencephalomalacia, the goat's brain of the goat becomes both edematous and inflamed. Typically, a ruminant would be somewhat resistant to this type of deficiency simply because it is capable of producing adequate amounts thiamin.

However, young ruminants and those eating a high grain diet are at risk. With the young goats, many do not have the ability to fight off this deficiency whereas high grain diets actually encourage the growth of some thiaminase-producing bacteria, which includes Clostridium Sporogenes, among others.

The result is that when a goat is faced with a thiamin deficiency, it can be harmful. Obviously, the best treatment is putting the goat on a proper diet. In some cases, it may be necessary to add thiamin supplements to the diet as a means of bringing the thiamin count back to normal.

Scours

Scours is a problem with diarrhea, typically associated with improper milk feeding or K99 strains of E. coli. To cure Scours in goats, there are two good options. The first is a product over the counter called Bar-Guard-99, which goat owners say works well.

Another solution is a home remedy that involves adding a dose of blackberry tea (made from leaves and roots of any blackberry plant) in the kid's milk or feeding it directly to the kid. The benefit of the home remedy is that the goat does not experience any side effects. In fact, in most cases the goat will show significant signs of improvement within five to seven days, if not sooner.

Scrapie

This degenerative disease affects a goat's central nervous system and unfortunately, is fatal. Scrapie falls under a category of diseases known as "transmissible spongiform encephalopathies" or TSE. If you have goats infected with Scrapie, typically your entire herd will be affected and over time, die.

Of all known viruses, the agent that causes Scrapie is the smallest. Although the exact nature of this disease is unknown, experts have narrowed the possibilities down to three. First, would be that the agent is actually a virus with unique characteristics, second that the agent is a prion, a type of protein in the brain that is malformed, and third, that the agent is a virino, which is a tiny piece of DNA that presents itself as a virus.

Typically, a goat with Scrapie will show symptoms in two to five years after being infected. Although the goat can live for a short while after becoming ill, death is imminent. Generally, you would notice the goat displaying tremors, struggling with coordination, experiencing behavioral changes, rubbing and/or scratching against hard objects such as a fence post, losing weight even though appetite is good, smacking its lips, walking with abnormal gaits, biting its limbs and feet, swaying its backend, and hopping like a rabbit.

What makes Scrapie so interesting is that on occasion, the goat will appear perfectly normal. The only indication in this situation that something is wrong is that any sudden noise or excitement would cause the goat stress at which time symptoms would surface. In fact, if the goat has Scrapie, once excited it could go into convulsions. Sadly, Scrapie has no known treatment so once a goat is infected, it would need to be destroyed.

Urinary Calculi

Calculi are crystals or stones that develop in the urinary tract of goats. This metabolic disease is actually common, seen primarily in kids eating diets comprised of high levels of ammonium phosphates, magnesium, and calcium. Since castrated kids are no longer influenced from hormones that develop the urinary tract, this illness is commonly seen in kids.

With Urinary Calculi, the crystals or stones become lodged, causing restriction and inflammation, as well as a blockage of flow in the urethra. With the inability to urinate properly, the goat will experience abdominal pain. If the problem is not corrected, the bladder or urethra could rupture, sometimes leading to death. If you have a goat with a distended or painful abdomen, notice it kicking at its belly, or seeing it try to urinate often, these could be indicators of a Urinary Calculi problem.

Urinary Tract Infection

For a goat with a urinary tract infection, antibiotics should be administered. For goats, this particular condition is commonly followed by urinary stones, which are very painful. In this case, the goat's feed should be changed to one that contains ammonium chloride to help acidify the urine and thus, prevent the development of crystals or stones.

Weak Legs

Sometimes, a kid will have weak hind legs that either fall behind the other legs or spread too far from the body. For a newborn kid, start by taking its temperature rectally to make sure it registers between 101.5 and 103.5. If the temperature is below 98 degrees, fill a tub or sink with warm water, immersing the kid to help raise the body temperature.

After a few minutes, retake the temperature and once it begins to climb closer to 100 degrees, remove the goat from the water, drying it off with a soft towel. Next, tube feed the kid with two ounces of warm colostrum, making sure it is healthy, being creamy and yellow in color.

Another problem associated with weak legs is a selenium deficiency. For older goats, the problem manifests as depression, weight loss, weak legs, and an overall condition of poor health. Sometimes referred to as White Muscle Disease, experts believe it could be caused by Nutritional Muscular Dystrophy.

Keep in mind that selenium is actually toxic. Therefore, when treating a goat for a selenium deficiency, you must be careful. In addition, selenium is controlled closely for feed so your best bet is to work with your veterinarian to get a confirmed diagnosis prior to obtaining treatment.

Administering Medication

As you read the above section, you probably wondered how oral medication should be administered to a goat. No need to worry - you have several options that will make the process easy. For example, you might consider drenching, which involves taking oral medication and then simply squirting it down the goat's throat.

To help with the process, use a drench gun. Although a standard syringe also works, the drench gun is specially designed for this purpose. This tool is made with a unique nozzle to control the direction of the medication and flow. In most cases, you would straddle the goat's neck and while using your legs to squeeze the chute, drench the goat. Do not be surprised when the goat lets out a loud noise of protest but remember you are not hurting it.

Vaccinations

Goats like many other animals are faced with a number of diseases as outlined in this chapter, although not all have been discussed. Before any medication is administered, talk with your veterinarian first. However, we have put some information together that could be used as a guide on when and what type of vaccinations the goat will need.

Bi-Annual

Twice a year, both doe and buck should be given CD/T and Bo-Se shots. In addition, the goat would be vaccinated one month prior to breeding and then one month before the due date of new kids.

Kid Vaccinations

At birth, give each kid 1/4 cc of Bo-Se. The kid would then receive on full vaccination of CD/T at five weeks, one full vaccination at 10 weeks, and then twice a year thereafter.

Disbudding

For buck kids, disbudding should be performed at two to three weeks for the miniature breeds and seven to ten days for dairy breeds. Then, at the time of disbudding, a tetanus anti-toxin shot should be administered.

Breeding, Pregnancy and Birth

In this chapter, we will discuss breeding, pregnancy, and the birth process of a goat. The information provided in this chapter is just a normal part of life. However, some of the discussions may be too graphic for young children. Therefore, we advise parents to read this chapter first and then decide if it is appropriate.

Breeding

Many people get involved with goats simply for breeding purposes. Whether looking to build a business for meat or dairy or breeding goats as pets, this makes a wonderful family project for everyone to enjoy. In most cases, a goat will have a heat cycle lasting anywhere from one or two days, up to 21 days. The heat cycle is more commonly seen in late August to mid March.

During heat, the goat will display a number of unique characteristics such as uneasiness, bleating, shaking the tail, and of course, riding other goats. Once the goat stops bleeding, the gestation period will begin. Typically, this phase starts from conception until birth, which is approximately 150 days. Keep in mind this timeframe is for dairy goats, varying vary among the different breeds.

A goat should not be bred until it reaches minimum of 85 pounds or 10 months of age. This rule is very important since early breeding tends to stunt the growth of the fetus, as well as the pregnant doe. When the doe gives birth, she will generally have two kids although three and sometimes four is relatively common. As far as gender, the ratio averages 115 males to 100 females.

Breeding a buck and doe is actually very easy. Bucks are virile and agile, often displaying sexual signs to entice and stimulate the doe. If successful, the doe will become excited and eager to mate. For the best breeding, provide your goats with a protected area so kids are not at risk of attack from wild animals such as coyotes, foxes, and wild dogs. In addition, the new kids and the doe will need a stall out of the cold with dry bedding.

Doe

The female goat, called a doe or nanny are seasonal breeders, meaning they come into heat sometime in the fall. As mentioned, a doe will mature sexually around five or six months of age but because breeding early can cause significant problems, you want her to be 85 pounds and at least 10 months of age. Although challenging you will need to be careful to keep the bucks away until she is ready.

Once the doe goes into heat, she will cycle every 17 days and then stay in heat for about one day although this can vary significantly. When the doe is big enough, old enough, and ready to breed, she will give out specific signs.

First, she will become very vocal. She will also begin urinating often, crouching down with her hind legs set apart. You will notice her fanning her tail and depending on the goat, she may try to get a little friendly with the owner or other goats.

As she becomes stimulated during her cycle, the smell of the buck will cause her to begin ovulation. Once the doe has been mounted and become pregnant, she will remain pregnant for around five months at which time she will deliver one, two, or three kids. Keep in mind that if you have a milking herd, you may have several females that display signs of pregnancy when in fact they are not.

Buck

The male goat is called the buck or billy. He reaches puberty around four to five months of age but even so, he may not yet be fertile. During a rut period, the male will omit a strong odor, which is made even worse by him spraying urine from an erect penis.

This spray falls on his underbelly, chest, and then onto his beard. As humans, we look at this behavior as disgusting but the doe loves it. This action, called enurination, occurs when the buck is tethered or kept in a separate stall from the doe while waiting to mate.

Another very odd behavior seen performed by the buck is a twisting of the body whereby he puts his own penis in his mouth, as the taste of the urine evokes a stimulating reaction. In fact, it is quite common for bucks to masturbate and then ejaculate on their underbelly and beard. Again, we do not understand this ritual but it is all a part of their natural behavior.

Just before the buck mounts the doe, he will investigate by sniffing her side and genital area. As he chases her around, he will make strange sounds, flicking his tongue in and out. If the doe should urinate, the buck will taste it, again giving a flehmen response. Before a successful mount is completed, the buck may make a couple false attempts.

Finally, he will mount her securely, ejaculating as he thrusts forward. He will then leap off the ground, consummating the relationship. During this process, the buck deposits billions of sperm just at the cervical opening.

The sperm must enter into the canal quickly in order to survive since the female goat's vagina is a very hostile environment for sperm. This process takes just a few minutes.

After the buck has ejaculated, it is common for him to clean off his penis, again displaying a stimulating response. As you can imagine, by the time mating season ends, the male goat smells horrible but as springtime approaches, there is excitement in the air about new kids' arrival.

Interesting Facts

For the sake of interest, we have provided a few interesting facts associated with breeding goats:

A full-grown buck in optimal physical condition can easily handle up to 25 doe during one mating season.

A kid buck also in great health can handle up to 10 doe in one mating season.

A kid, whether male or female, can be fertile by the age of seven weeks. Now, you would certainly not breed a goat this young but if you did, it could produce.

For breeding purposes, there are two types of goats – Equatorial and Alpine:

Equatorial – These goats come from regions where the climate is hot all year round. In addition, the Equatorial goats are year round breeders.

Alpine – The Alpine is primarily a dairy goat, which is a seasonal breeder that usually breeds from August to late December to early January.

Pregnancy

Pregnancy in goats is maintained by the hormone progesterone. With sheep pregnancies, the progesterone is first produced by the corpus luteum, which is the structure formed on the ovary whenever an egg is shed, and then in the last portion of the pregnancy, the placenta. With a goat, the only source of progesterone throughout the entire pregnancy is the corpus luteum.

Since stress can easily upset the function of the corpus luteum causing natural abortion, it is very important for the doe to be kept calm and comfortable. You want to keep loud cars and trucks away from the pregnant doe, stop dogs from running near the stall or in the pasture, use the lawnmower at a good distance, and so on.

Gestation

The standard gestation for a goat is between 145 and 155 days. Keep in mind that some breeds have a kid early while some go late. Therefore, these dates are merely averages. The best rule of thumb is to count 150 days from the time the goat was bred, expecting that the kids could arrive one week prior.

Knowing if a doe is pregnant can be challenging. Typically, if pregnant, she would not go into another heat but other than that, the only sure way of confirming pregnancy is with ultrasound. If an ultrasound is chosen, it will tell you how far along the pregnancy is, the location of the fetus, the size of the fetus, and sometimes, if the doe is carrying more than one kid.

As mentioned, a doe usually has one or two kids but when breeding is done in late fall, the chance of three or four kids is improved. Remember, a female goat can look and act pregnant without being pregnant. In fact, this is commonly seen with a herd of milking goats.

In addition, a pregnant goat may not even show for a full month before ready to give birth, and some will not show at all. For this reason, it is crucial that the 150-day countdown be done at the time of breeding. If this will be the goat's first pregnancy, sometime around four to six weeks prior to birth, she will begin making her udder.

At this time, the udder would not fill with milk and colostrum until days prior to the birth. However, if the doe has had a kid previously, her udder would begin filling about one week prior to birth. These are just averages to give you an idea of what to expect.

One important note – since you cannot be 100% certain about the birthing date, it is important that a doe never be housed with bucks. While some will do fine together, you never know when the buck will turn mean, harming both doe and new kid. Therefore, it is always better to be on the safe side by keeping them separate.

Production Years

A doe will continue going into heat and produce kids throughout her entire life. Unlike women who go through the change of life whereby they are no longer capable of producing children, a goat keeps having baby as long as she lives. Typically, a goat will live anywhere from 11 to 13 years and as long as she is put with a buck during her heat cycle, she will have babies until she dies of old age.

Now, remember that breeding and kidding an older doe is one cause of early death. Therefore, if your female goat is a family pet that you want around for years to come, she should stop being bred around the age of seven or eight. At this point, make sure she is not exposed to a buck. By retiring your doe, her life span can actually be extended to 17 or 20 years!

After the doe kids, she will eventually go into a new heat cycle. Even so, you should wait to breed her again since birthing and feeding a new baby takes tremendous effort and energy on her part. The new mother needs time to rest, breeding her just one time per year. Additionally, just because a mother goat is nursing does not protect her from becoming pregnant. In fact, while milking, a doe can pregnant easier.

Problems in Pregnancy

Sometimes, a pregnant doe will experience problems while pregnant. In this section, we will discuss some of the more common risks, as well as proper treatment options.

Selenium Deficiency

As mentioned earlier, selenium deficiency can create significant problems for goats. This mineral is found naturally in the earth but sometimes if goats are raised in regions where levels of selenium are low, the deficiency comes into play. If you live in such an area, your veterinarian may recommend your pregnant goat (along with other goats) be given an injection of Bo-Se.

Toxemia

Toxemia is something that even humans can develop. In goats, toxemia, also known as ketosis, can be fatal. This condition appears in the final five weeks of the doe's pregnancy or soon after freshening. Either way, Toxemia is extremely dangerous and even deadly. The key here is early detection. With proper treatment, the doe and fetus can be saved.

Toxemia is neither form of bacteria or virus. Instead, this condition is a nutritional deficiency that typically occurs within five weeks of delivery. If the goat has Toxemia, she would present with depression, lethargy or dullness, and a lack of appetite. As the conditions worsen, symptoms will progress to include an overall weakness and difficulty walking, if walking at all.

Once the symptoms of Toxemia develop, they can progress quickly. In fact, you might at first notice the doe sitting down but rising without problem. However, as the problem becomes more severe, the doe would find it hard to get up from a sitting position.

If the doe reaches this stage of the illness without treatment, chances are it is too late to reverse the devastating effects. Therefore, if you have a pregnant doe, watch for signs of Toxemia around the five-week to delivery mark.

When Toxemia is diagnosed and treated early, it can be met with great success. Typically, a urine test such as a Keto-check would be performed, which is highly accurate. Once the condition is confirmed, treatment would involve the administration of propylene glycol, which is non-toxic to goats. If you are unable to perform testing yourself and you notice signs of Toxemia, propylene glycol can be administered as a precautionary measure.

Although you cannot always stop the development of Toxemia, there are steps that can be taken for prevention. One method is to provide the doe with top dressing in the feed late in her pregnancy consisting of molasses or sugar. In fact, adding molasses to the drinking water for any pregnant doe ensures she is getting adequate nutrition, with or without signs of Toxemia.

The diet of a pregnant doe should consist of high quality roughage along with increased concentrates. If you suspect Toxemia, offer the goat exercise, even forced if necessary. In addition, consider providing the doe with high-energy supplements to keep her from becoming ketotic.

Some of the best treatment options include nutria-drench, dextrose, TKM solution, magic (one part molasses, two parts Kayro syrup, and one part corn oil), and finally, glucose IV.

Chlamydiosis

If you have tried to raise kids but for some reason they are consistently stillborn, it is possible that Chlamydiosis is occurring in the last two months of the doe's pregnancy. Keep in mind that this is just one possibility but something to investigate.

With this, the key to controlling Chlamydiosis has to do with the time during the pregnancy when she becomes infected. If Chlamydiosis occurs early on, the result would be an aborted fetus or a full-term but stillborn kid. On occasion, a pregnant doe with Chlamydiosis will deliver kids that have lesions. In this case, the placenta should be retained and shown to a veterinarian to determine the exact cause.

Worms

Unfortunately, even a pregnant doe must deal with worms. When thinking about breeding a female goat, it would be a good idea to deworm her prior to the breeding or soon after kidding. This will help with the prevention of egg production.

If a deworming process needs to be completed prior to kidding, make sure the product is guaranteed to be safe during pregnancy. For the dewormer to be effective, the female goat's weight must be accurate. If an entire herd will be dewormed, calculate the appropriate dose according to the heaviest goat's weight.

The problem is that if the dose of deworming medication is too low, you will be faced with resistance from the parasites. Just remember that whatever the prescribed dosage, experts recommend you administer 1.5 times that for goats.

Sore Udders

Many times, goats will develop sore udders caused from kid's suckling. To provide the doe with some relief while making sure the kid will not ingest anything harmful, choose the products wisely. One option that works quite well is called Molly's Marvelous Herbal Salve. Applied directly to the teats, the goat will enjoy the soothing sensation the salve provides.

Although typically used for sore udders, this product is multifunctional. For example, the salve can be used to provide the goat relief form bug bites, dry skin, cuts or scrapes, and fungal infection. Additionally, this salve is great to ease the pain and promote healing of disbudding.

Vaccinations, Dewormers, Medication

The products below will guide you in treating a pregnant doe for instances of worms, vaccinations, diseases, and so on.

Bo-Se

This medication is used to prevent health problems in new kids. Generally, Bo-Se would be measured at 1/2ml, which should be administered two weeks prior to birth. Since the main purpose of Bo-Se is to replenish selenium, it is important to check with your veterinarian prior to medicating to determine if your area has a selenium deficiency. The reason this is important is that if there is no deficiency and Bo-Se were given, it could actually cause selenium poisoning.

Covexin - 8

Given as 2ml SQ followed by a booster of 2ml SQ in 21 days, this medication is safe for a pregnant doe in treating both Type C and Type D Enterotoxemia (an overeating disease). Then two weeks prior to kidding, the doe would need to be revaccinated. Other uses of this medication include 7-Way Blackleg and Tetnus.

Fresh Cow YMCP Plus

This product is a combination of calcium, betaine, niacin, magnesium, yeast, and potassium, all substances needed by a doe after kidding. In addition, Fresh Cow YMCP Plus will help the doe transition from the kidding phase to the lactating phase.

Ivomec

This dewormer helps control immature and mature stages of external and internal parasites. A good, all-around product, Ivomec works well on common worms such as grubs, lung worms, round worms, mange mites, and sucking lice. For the pregnant doe, Ivomec has been found safe. The dosage would be 1ml per 50 pounds of weight.

Lactated Ringer Solution

If a goat needs electrolytes or rehydration, this would be a good product to use. The standard dosage is 30cc SQ injected.

Lepto-5

This medication is also safe for pregnant goats, preventing Lepto-Spirosis, which includes five separate types that include Leptospira Canicola, L. Hardio, L. Grippotyphosa, L. Pomona, and Icterohaemorrhagiae. This particular vaccination consists of inactivated whole cultures of each of these five.

The L. Pomona is the particular strain that can cause an abortion in goats. For dosage, administer 2ml once the kids are two months old. Then four weeks later, the doe would be given a 2ml booster.

In addition, it is a good idea to administer 2ml one week prior to breeding the goat and then two weeks after kidding. The buck should also be vaccinated prior to breeding to ensure nothing bad is passed on to the doe.

Levasole

Some veterinarians feel this dewormer is safe for a pregnant doe while other vets are not convinced. Therefore, prior to administering Levasole, it would be best to discuss potential risks with your personal veterinarian.

Liquamycin LA-200

Of all antibiotics, this is the hardest working and longest lasting. Although commonly used for Pinkeye and pneumonia, Liquamycin LA-200 is also used for lactating goats. Sometimes, a goat will become ill after giving birth.

In this case, Liquamycin LA200 would be a viable option. Unfortunately, this injectable antibiotic is painful so you will need to keep the goat calm during and after the injection.

Lutalyse

This particular medication is used for estrus synchronization and treatment of silent heats. For example, if you need to encourage heat in your goat, administer 2ml regardless of the breed.

Now, if you have a doe that bred too young and therefore, the fetus needs to be aborted, you would administer 2ml immediately after the breeding occurred. For this, the abortion will usually occur within 18 hours after the injection is given.

Probios Gel

This medication works well for sick goats. If your doe has given birth and needs her appetite stimulated, Probios Gel would be a consideration. Other benefits include improving digestion and reducing stress associated with weaning kids.

Safe Guard

Safe Guard is safe for goats. Even though this medication consists of a 10% Fenbendazole paste, no milk withdrawal is required. Since some goats have built up immunity to this dewormer, you should talk to your veterinarian prior to administering. If the veterinarian approves of this treatment, it is important the goat's mouth be void of any food while Safe Guard is being administered.

Tramisol

This is not a safe product for pregnant goats. Therefore, it should be avoided.

Valbazen

This is not a safe product for pregnant goats. Therefore, it should be avoided.

Vitamin B Complex

Used as a nutritional supplement, Vitamin B complex provides a doe with a much-needed boost of energy. Often, birth will cause weakness, making the goat susceptible to infection. Given in a dose from 3cc to 5cc, vitamin B complex improves overall health and appetite.

Goat Nutri-Drench

This product is excellent for the doe that has just given birth. Loaded with vitamins A, D, and E, along with amino acids, glucose, and trace minerals, the doe will have far more energy. Typically, given as an oral medication, the effects of this medication is quick.

After the initial dose, repeat treatment every eight to ten hours as needed, using an oral application of one ounce of medicine per 100 pound of goat. For the newborn kids, 4cc should be administered immediately after birth.

Reproductive System

To gain more information about breeding goats and the reproductive system for each breed, we would recommend you utilize any of the following resources:

Goat Connection – www.goatconnection.com

PCM Consulting - www.pcmconsulting.com.au/goats

Goat World -
http://www.goatworld.com/articles/meatgoatbreeds.shtml

Kidding

Kidding, also known as parturition, occurs as the female goat prepares to give birth. This phase of birth could be compared with labor that a woman ensures. For example, some women will have labor that lasts a few hours whereas other women can go on for days. The same is true for goats in that the kidding phase varies from one goat to another.

Preparing for Birth

Most goat breeders highly recommend that you be present during the actual birth. Having counted out the 150 days from breeding and then one week back, you will know exactly when to prepare for the newborn.

Start by placing the doe in a separate stall with dry, clean bedding, good food, and clean water. Make sure the stall has plenty of fresh air but no drafts. As the time approaches, keep your eyes open for the signs of birth to include anxiousness and even a change in her appearance.

The doe's tail ligaments are located on both sides of her spine about halfway between the location where the back slopes downward and her tail. These ligaments should be checked often in that as the impending birth gets closer, they will soften and become loose.

At first, these ligaments will feel similar to pencils. However, as time passes, you will begin to notice a change. Run your hand down the back of the doe, checking for any telltale signs. As the ligaments start to change, you will also notice the goat's back start to arch just above the tail. In fact, the tail itself will start to rise.

To ensure no problems arise during birth, it is common for goat breeders to place an audio and/or video monitor in the stall. This way, should there be any changes in the middle of the night of if the doe were to have difficulties then they would be aware and able to take appropriate action.

Birthing Kit

Now, as birth begins, it is beneficial to have a birthing kit prepared. Several days prior to the expected birth, this kit should be organized and ready to go. Typically, a goat will give birth on her, void of any problems. Unfortunately, there are occasions when the doe needs a little bit of assistance. The items listed below should be included in your birthing kit – just in case!

Antiseptic lubricant to assist in retrieving the kid from the doe's womb

Baby bottle with a Prichard teat to help the kid eat if it has difficulty in the beginning

Contact information for the veterinarian

Dental floss, which can be used to tie off the umbilical cord

Empty feed bags for the doe to deliver her kids on

Flashlight to check the kid's position and progress of the birth. Simply shine the light up through the bubble.

Goat sweaters for the doe if she delivers in chilly weather

Quiet hairdryer for drying off the kid

Iodine 7% Tincture for sterilizing the scissors (or knife)

Large garbage bag to hold the soiled bags, paper towels, afterbirth, and so on

Paper towel for wiping off the new babies

Puppy housetraining pads to place the wet kids, which are soft and highly absorbent

Scissors to burst the bubble and to cut the kid's umbilical cord

Small jars to hold the iodine for dipping the navels

Surgical hand scrub just in case the doe needs help with brining out the kid

Warm water for washing up

Weak lamb syringe to encourage the kid to eat

After the Birth

After the birth, certain things happen naturally. Some occur immediately and some take days. Regardless, the list below provides you with a list of what you should expect to happen.

Bottom of the kid's hooves will shed the protective white coating (soon after birth)

Kids will urinate and have a first stool, which will be black and tar-like (soon after birth)

Kid's stool will become soft and mustard-like (for about one week after birth)

Legs will straighten completely and the kid will begin to walk properly (could take a few days and depending on the success, the kid may require a shot of Bo-Se)

Afterbirth will be delivered after the birth (only one placenta per kid and sometimes, one per kidding). Many times, the doe will eat the afterbirth, which is actually normal and healthy for her.

Doe will ooze blood and mucous after birth, which is normal (occurs for two to three weeks after birth)

Newborn Kids

The kidding is considered complete after the doe has given birth, cleaned the babies, and accepted them to nurse. Although it might be tempting, never pick up the newborn kid until around one month of age. Picking up newborn kids too early creates risk that the doe will not accept her babies.

Since kids are born in the spring when there is plenty of fresh food, the doe is usually capable of providing all the milk needed by the kid. While some people believe that supplementary feeding of the doe during pregnancy is important, studies have been conducted that do not support this. In fact, studies show that supplemental milk has nothing to do with the kid's weight at birth or degree of survival.

On average, a newborn male will average 3.5 pounds and 3.1 pounds for twins. For female kids, the average weight for a single baby is 3.0 pounds and for twins 2.8 pounds. In both cases, the mortality rate is less than 10%. In either case, these tiny creatures at birth are absolutely, adorable.

Both doe and her new babies should remain in the same stall for up to two weeks, providing the perfect opportunity for mother and child to bond without being bothered by other goats. During this time, the kid will be able to nurse all it wants. On about the second day, both doe and babies should be taken outside for about an hour to get fresh air, as long as it is sunny and warm.

Keep in mind that a doe without kids is not interested in being around new babies. In fact, other female goats will push the kids aside gently, swish their tail, or in some other way, make it know to the new kids to back off. Over time, the new kids can be introduced to the rest of the goats at which time they should do fine.

Four Days Old

When the kids reach four days old, they will need to be given a dose of Probios. Provide room for play that might include some wood or cement blocks to climb on, and start socializing them. Within the first four days, kids will need to be disbudded and although not a fun process, it is important.

Two Weeks Old

When the kids reach two weeks of age, they will be with the other goats all the time, playing and having a great time. Keep in mind that you want to put the baby goats in their own stall at night, offering them clean, warm bedding, fresh grain, and water.

Then in the mornings, milk the doe, leaving just enough for the kids to suckle. Once milked, the babies can rejoin the doe to nurse and continue bonding until nighttime when they will again be placed in a private stall.

Three Weeks Old

At about three weeks of age, the kids will need the first CD&T vaccination. In addition, the Coccidiosis prevention treatment should be started. At this age, the male kids should be wethered, also known as neutered.

You want to wait until three weeks of age for this process to allow ample time for the pee hole to grow large enough to eliminate the risk of stones. While some people use the rubber band method, known as banding, this is actually painful to the goat. Therefore, you might consider a different method called "burdizo".

The goal is to avoid any cutting that could potentially create a wound just asking for infection. Instead, by using the burdizo, the wethering is quick. In fact, the kids are up playing in about an hour or so in most cases.

Four Weeks to Two Months Old

By four weeks of age, the kids will be put on a worming schedule to control the invasion of parasites. Then at six weeks, the kids will need a CD&T booster along with their second treatment for Coccidiosis.

Finally, by the time the kids reach two months of age, they will again go on a schedule for wormwood. At this age, they will be ready to leave the rest of the goats. If you plan to sell the kids, make sure they are a minimum of eight weeks old and fully weaned.

Problems after Birth

In this section, you will learn about some of the common problems seen after the kid is born.

Non-Nursing Kid

Sometimes, a baby goat will not nurse off its mother's teats, as it should. With newborn kids, you want to watch for a bobbing head as the baby searches for food. Start by squeezing the teats of the doe to ensure her milk is in.

Typically, you can gently guide the kid back to the mother's teats to take its first meal. Simply point the kid's face toward the teat, allowing allow some of the milk to drop down on its face/mouth.

If you try to force the situation, the kid will become afraid and the doe frustrated. Therefore, it is far better to take the situation one-step at a time. Usually, just a few drops of milk into or near the kid's mouth would be enough to entice it to the teats.

During this process, you need to remain calm and be patient, keeping the mother calm and encouraged. If necessary, you can offer her some top grain or even a small handful of raisins. Once the kid begins to suckle, it will need little coaxing.

Depending on the mother goat, she may or may not like nursing while she herself is eating. In this case, when the kid is hungry, remove the goats feed just until the kid has finished eating. Again, offer her a special treat as a reward for her patience so she learns to put her baby first.

Another common situation involves the mother getting involved with cleaning her baby. In fact, when this occurs, the doe will be so focused that she is unable to stand still long for the kid to nurse. To help with this situation, hold the kid so its behind is within reach of the doe. While holding her collar to prevent her from turning around, the kid can eat.

Although this does not occur often, sometimes a doe will be nervous about giving birth, being a mom, and having a baby nursing on her teats. In this case, she will move around, try to kick, or start jumping as a way of getting "that thing" away from her. This situation requires a lot of patience on your behalf.

Start by holding her by the collar while holding the kid by her udder. On occasion, the mother will immediately understand her role and everything comes together beautifully. However, you will find that sometimes trying to help the kid nurse can make the situation worse. The key here is for the doe to see and smell her little one. She needs to understand that she can lick her baby while the baby goes to her udder.

Slowly work with both the doe and her kid until both understand the nursing process. If an hour passes with no success, milk the doe so the kid can be fed with a bottle. Simply place the baby in your lap, allowing it to suckle for a nice teaser.

After tasting the milk, the kid will obviously not be satisfied. At this time, guide it back to the doe's teat to see if things will happen naturally. This process may take several attempts until it finally clicks for mother and baby. On rare occasions, the mother will not accept the kid at all. If you are faced with this situation, the kid or kids will need to be bottle -fed.

Now, if you end up bottle-feeding the babies, you can purchase a special nipple called a Pritchard flutter valve nipple, specifically designed for baby goats. Start by feeding the kid three times a day, helping it become accustomed to "nursing" whenever it wants. From three, you can keep the kid on this schedule or change it to twice a day, depending on the appetite.

With this, you want to continue feeding the kid, keeping the milk intake at no more than one quart a day, although you may need to be a little bit flexible depending on the kid. For example, if the kid is a little premature, you might need to stick with the three times a day schedule or even increase it to four.

Mastitis

As discussed earlier, Mastitis is inflammation of the mammary glands caused by bacteria. For the new mother with Mastitis, she will be experiencing pain, swelling, and heat of the udder. Obviously, when the kid goes to nurse, this becomes too much to bear.

Sometimes, Mastitis will involve a blackish color of the teats and slight discharge. To treat Mastitis, the udder would need to be milked and rubbed repeatedly to promote a natural flow of the milk. In addition, the doe should be treated with antibiotics to bring the infection under control while keeping the Mastitis from spreading.

Disbudding

Disbudding involves the removing of the kid's horns. This procedure is usually carried out to ensure the goats do not harm one another as they age. For dairy goats to be registered, disbudding is a requirement. In addition, many Boer goats to be sold at market must also be disbudded.

If disbudding is not performed correctly, it can be a very painful procedure for the goat. Therefore, it is essential that you be a responsible goat owner, choosing the method least painful. If you are not comfortable disbudding the kids, a qualified veterinarian can do the job. Remember, disbudding is best done on young goats.

One of the more common techniques is known as the "elastrator method". With this, the goat is not stressed although some people disagree. Bands are placed around each of the goat's horns using elastrator pliers.

Next, the bands are rolled up as close as possible to the skull. Duct tape is applied to the front of the horns to eliminate the bands from being rubbed off by the goat. The elastrator band cuts off blood circulation going from the skull to the horn.

The bands work by closing in on the soft tissue part of the horn, eventually severing it. If the goat is older when disbudded, the horn will begin to change shape, become brittle, and fall off. If the horn does not fall off naturally, then blunt force is required to remove it.

Weaning

The best option for weaning is to allow the doe to raise her own kids. Generally, you would do nothing regarding the weaning process, allowing the doe to choose when it is time to kick the kids off the teats. In fact, your interference could make both doe and her kids feel uncomfortable and stressed.

Allowing the mother to wean her babies is both natural and the most successful method. If f the kids were being bottle raised, then you would start the weaning process around three months of age.

Friendly Kids

If your goal for having goats is to keep or sell them as pets, they will need to be socialized at an early age. To ensure the goats grow into well-adjusted and friendly adults, the kids must be loved, played with, and cuddled. For years, people believed the only way to have a friendly buck or doe was to bottle-feed them as babies but today, we know socialization if far more important.

The interesting aspect of this is that long-time breeders completely disagree. In fact, they state that many of the bottle-fed babies actually grow up to be less friendly and social than the goats nursed by the doe. Therefore, the primary concern is on handling the kids often, teaching them that humans are good. Although this might take a little more time, the result is a warm and affectionate animal.

Proper Handling

It is important to know how to handle goats correctly. Goats actually have a spot where they love being petted, located on the side of the neck near the chin. They also love having their armpits and breastbone petted.

Just as they have their favorite spots, goats also have a spot where they do not like to be petted – the top of the head. For some reason, petting on the top of the head makes them feel nervous and defensive. Rather than reaching toward the goat, hold your hand in front of its neck. With this, the goat can follow your hand, gaining confidence in your handling.

Approachability

While the mother goat is out grazing in the pasture, take the opportunity to spend time with the kids. Allow the babies to approach you first so they can explore and feel comfortable around you. Do not reach out to touch or handle the kids until they are ready. Sometimes, the kids will begin to nibble on your clothing or push up against you, which are good signs. Keep in mind that kids need time to work out their curiosity.

As kids become more and more confident with you, they will approach you more freely, even climbing on your lap. At this point, you can gently reach over, pick one up, and hold it closely. As you pet the goat, talk to it in a loving and soothing voice.

At first, the kid may try to wiggle free. In this case, hold it closely while petting and talking. With patience and determination, you will soon have a special relationship with the kids. The goal is to let the kids know you will not harm them, thus building up trust.

If you have a kid that is very unsure about getting too close, you might offer a snack of raisins. Kids love raisins, doing just about anything to get them. Start by holding the raisins in your hands, letting the kid get a whiff. Then, squeeze the raisins slightly so your hands have both smell and taste of raisins. As the kid gets closer, let it lick your hand. Next, open your hand with raisins so the kid will come closer. This works so well that many people keep raisins with them at all times, finding them to be a magical treat!

Buying and Caring For a Goat

If you have some land and are interested in adding goats to the family, this chapter will address some of the things you need to know. Just as with little kittens or puppies, baby goats are absolutely, adorable. They have the sweetest face in the world, making them easy to love.

Owning goats is a great thing but it also requires responsibility. As cute as goats are, it would be easy to go home with a whole bunch of kids, forgetting that they eventually grow into adults. Therefore, before you hurry out to buy goats, understand the responsibility and requirements associated with owning one (or more).

Obviously, goats require a clean place to live, dry, fresh bedding, good grain food, and fresh water. In addition, goats need to be checked at least twice a day. In fact, during the cold winter months, goats should be checked more often. In addition to the responsibility of food, water, and housing, you also need to consider the cleaning, shoveling manure, scrubbing out water troughs, trimming feet, brushing hair, administering medication, and all the other aspects of owning goats.

Unfortunately, some people get so excited about the prospect of owning a goat that they forget or simply overlook what happens when you want to go on vacation. Because goats need consistent care, you would need a responsible person to care for your pets while gone. In addition, prior to buying goats you want to check with your local laws to ensure goats are permitted where you live. If you live on land but are included in a homeowner's association, they may not permit goats. For this reason, always make sure owning a goat is an option where you live prior to making the investment.

Always remember that goats are vocal characters. Therefore, if you have nearby neighbors that do not appreciate noise, owning a goat could present some problems. For this reason, before buying always consider housing, fencing, care, veterinarian bills, and every aspect possible. Although there are many things to consider and owning a goat is a big responsibility, you can be sure these wonderful creatures will enhance your life and keep you laughing!

The Right Goat

When choosing your goat, remember that one breed is not necessarily better than another breed. However, some goats are better suited for certain situations than other goats. For example, if you want a goat to produce milk, choose any of the **milking goats** listed above. The one considered the best all-around goat is the Nubian, although they all have wonderful characteristics.

If you want goats only for **meat**, then choose a breed from the list of meat producing goats. Perhaps you want goats that can be used for their fine **hair**. In this case, choose the appropriate breed. With the Angora or Cashmere goat, hair can be woven into fine apparel and home textiles. Finally, if you want a good family pet, the two best choices would be the Pygmy and the Nubian. Again, the final decision is yours to make but your success will depend largely on how well you choose.

When you get ready to buy, look over the many different **breeds** of goats as discussed earlier to determine the breed best for you. Miniature goats are the most adorable goat in the world. They are extremely loving, very affectionate, and a great choice. However, the miniature goat does not like being left alone. For this reason, if you decide to buy a miniature goat, you need to be in a position of being home. In addition, most goats prefer to be with other goats so you might consider buying two, possible three.

Pygmy

Although there are many wonderful breeds, one of the most popular goats to keep as a family pet is the Pygmy. This breed is a favorite because it is inexpensive, easy to care for, makes a great family pet, and can be used for showing. Although small, the Pygmy is hardy with a huge personality

The downfall to the Pygmy goat is that it cannot be house-broken, meaning you would need to provide a space approximately 8 x 10 feet. In addition to housing, the Pygmy also needs room to run and play in a fenced, secure area.

Although you would provide your pet goat with an occasional brushing, warm bath, and hoof trim every six weeks, this goat needs very little grooming. For diet, this breed typically eats sweet food and roughage. When feeding Pygmy goats or any goat for that matter, make sure they have the right types of plants and trees since some are poisonous to goats.

The Pygmy goat will live to the age of nine or ten. When at maturity, it will measure just between 16 and 23 inches long. Depending on the registration and show quality of the goat, you would expect to pay anywhere from $75 to $500! It is important to understand that the buck Pygmy often has a distinct odor and will appear more aggressive than the female.

The only real concern in owning a Pygmy goat is that this breed can develop a genetic condition known as spastic paresis. With this, the goat would experience muscle spasms in the hind legs. In addition, although this goat is small, it is very sly, quickly learning ways to jump or climb over fences. Therefore, proper housing is essential.

Nubian

Nubian goats were originally called Dwarf Nubian goats because they are the cross between a Nigerian Dwarf (buck) and a Nubian goat (doe). Although not a true miniature, the Nubian goat has a slight convex nose, short stature of 19 to 26 inches, a stocky body, medium length coat, and cute pendulous ears.

Although many people buy the Nubian goat for milk due to high production (up to six pounds a day), this breed of goat also makes an excellent pet. The Nubian is easy to care for and handle, making it a nice choice for family pet. Most people agree that this breed has a certain elegance and style that you do not see with other breeds.

If you have children that need a fun and easy to handle goat for a 4-H project, the Nubian goat would be ideal. This breed is also perfect for elderly people wanting to raise goats without putting a great deal of effort into the process. This goat needs very little space and is a year-round breeder. Very people oriented and gentle, you cannot go wrong choosing a Nubian goat.

Behavior

Most of the miniature breeds are overly friendly. They have excellent temperaments, thus making great pets. As with any goat, the kids should be held while young and even bottle-feed on occasion to help socialize them.

The funny thing about goats is that they love human companionship. For this reason, they will often bond closely with members of the family. Most experts say that goats cannot be potty trained although there have been reports of a few goat owners having succeed. If you want to try to train your goat to do tricks, food rewards are the best enticement.

To keep the goat's temperament even keeled, always avoid rough housing of any kind. If you have children, they will need to be taught the importance of handling the goats with love and tender care. If you have a dog, it too will need to be introduced to the goat, allowing time for the two to become friends. Since goats generally do not like being alone, it is highly recommended you keep two or three.

While surprising, desexed (wethered) male goats actually make the better gender for a pet. The reason is that females are always in their heat cycle, making them more unsettled. In addition, the desexed males do not have a foul odor like males that are not neutered. If you still want a female, it is recommended you keep two females or one female and a wethered male.

The Right Number

After choosing the right goat for your specific needs, you now have the decision of how many goats you want. Again, it is highly recommend that you have two or more but understand this will depend primarily on the amount of land available.

A good rule to follow is that for every one acre, you could easily accommodate between seven and ten goats. The key in choosing the number also depends on the quantity and quality of forage the land offers. Remember, goats are better browsers than they are grazers, meaning they need trees and brush rather than just grass.

Goats and Other Animals

Goats usually get along quite well with other animals such as cows, horses, donkeys, and sheep. Goats and dogs can also get along if they are introduced early and watched until all signs of problems are gone. The only concern here is that a dog, especially if you have several, will work in packs, sometimes becoming aggressive toward the goats.

Goats and pigeons, chickens, and other birds can be a problem in that the birds will drop feces in the goat's drinking water, causing them to become ill. Finally, when it comes to pigs, there are some diseases passed down from pigs that can be harmful to goats. Therefore, talk to your veterinarian prior to putting goats and pigs in the same pasture.

Determining Age

When buying your goat, you want to know its age. To do this, look at the eight, lower front teeth. Keep in mind that goats do not have any upper front teeth, instead merely gumming their food opposed to chewing it. Realize that the age will only be an estimate since each goat is a little different. For example, you might see one goat that has teeth that grow but then fall out, not providing a true age. In addition, the teeth of the various breeds will be slightly different. To help, use the following guidelines:

Kid (First Year)

The teeth will all be small but very sharp

Goatling/Yearling (Second Year)

For this age, the two middle front teeth will fall out sometime around one year at which time they replaced with larger, permanent teeth

Two-Year-Old (Third Year)

The teeth located to the middle pair are replaced with permanent teeth sometime around age two

Three-Year-Old (Fourth Year)

For the four-year-old, the goat will now have six permanent teeth but just one pair of kid teeth left

Four-Year-Old (Fifth Year)

The goat now has a set of eight front teeth

Over Five Years

Once the goat is around five years old, age is determined primarily by the wear of the teeth. This can be tricky since a number of factors will have an effect on the teeth such as diet, health, and so on. Additionally, goats that eat coarse diets along with rough pasture food will generally grind their teeth faster than a goat on hay and softer grain.

As the goat ages past age five, the teeth will begin to loosen and spread out until they finally just fall out.

Hoof Trimming

Goats need to have their hooves trimmed about every two months. Like a human's fingernails, the hooves will grow quickly and if not trimmed, they can bend, crack and even become badly infected. To trim your goat's hooves, you first want to make sure any dirt has been cleaned out using a hoof pick.

Now, using the trimmers, trim off the side of the wall for each hoof, followed by the heel working downward to each hoof is even and flat with the sole of the foot, also called the "frog". Be very careful only to trim down to where you begin to see pink. If you go any further, you will cut too deeply, causing bleeding.

Next, any excess hoof between the two heel areas would be trimmed. If you find the wall of the hoof starting to separate from the hood, this will need to be trimmed off completely to open it up and clean it out. These dirty pockets are havens for infection so make sure no dirt has been left that could cause problems such as foot rot.

The timing for trimming the hooves will depend on the breed and sometimes, the specific goat. For example, some goats may only need to have their hooves trimmed three to four times each year. However, if the goat spends a lot of time in the pasture, climbing, playing on rocks, and so on, then the feet may not need to be trimmed as often.

To determine if the feet need to be trimmed, look at the back hooves. The reason is that the front hooves will naturally wear down faster and thereby not need to be trimmed as often as the back hooves. When you do trim, wear gloves to avoid cutting yourself or developing blisters from the trimmers. Keep in mind that hooves can be thick so there may be times when you need to use a little bit of pressure, which can be hard on the hands.

Below is a list recommended trimmers but no matter the brand that you choose, just make sure they are sharp. That way, the trimmers are doing the work for you, providing a nice, clean cut. Before you begin trimming the hooves, wash the feet down so you can see what you are doing better. In addition, it would help to have something like a milk stand handy to hold the goat while you do the trimming. If the goat is nervous, offer it some grain or treats to keep it distracted.

Finally, if your goat struggles during the trimming process, to ensure she does not try to roll or lie down, place a bucket under her belly. The most important thing is to take your time. Some goats will go through the trimming process without any stress at all while other goats become very agitated. Therefore, learn how your goat reacts and be prepared to react accordingly. If the goat's feet are in bad shape, then you should take it to your veterinarian for assistance.

Training

Goats are actually very intelligent animals. With patience and proper training, this animal can be taught to perform tricks. The time you would have to invest in training your goat would depend on several factors to include the type of goat you have, the level of training and your skill level as a trainer.

As an example, the miniature goats are very gentle and easy to handle. Because of that, they are easy to work with whereas some of the other goats meant for meat are not as capable. Even so, with time and effort, you might be amazed at what you can accomplish.

When showing goats, they are required to wear a collar, halter, or chain. Now, with halter breaking, this is a great way to begin the training process, particularly if you have more than one goat. When going through many of the training options, the goat would need to be kept in the halter, collar, or chain and then tied to a fence. The goat here is to tie the goat where you can work with it and not where it will be injured during the process. Most importantly, never leave your goat tied and unattended.

Once the goat has become quiet and gentle use the halter, collar, or chain to keep its head up. Then, you can have a family member or friend help by pushing the goat from behind while you gently pull on the lead, teaching it to walk on a leash. The key is to teach your goat to lead with the front shoulder while staying even with your leg and the goat's head in front of your body.

Next, set up the front legs of the goat first, followed by placing the hind legs. While doing this, you want to keep the neck and body perfectly, straight with the head held high and proud. To do this, you can use the assistance of the halter, chain, or collar. While training your goat, always remain in a standing position, never kneeling or squatting down.

Once you have completed the training session with your goat, go through practice runs as if actually showing. Make sure the goat looks great and responds properly. As soon as the goat does what it is supposed to do, consider it a day. After taking it back to the pen, offer the goat a nice treat. If you were showing in the real world, you would be on a set time so the goat would have to respond quickly. Therefore, as you train your goat, you need to work with a set time.

Recommended Trimmers

Shear Magic – These trimmers cost around $17. Very compact, lightweight, and designed with an easy action handle, goat owners love them. The blades are made from sharp Teflon so every cut is clean and fast.

Jeffers Foot Rot Shears – Averaging $10, these shears are 10 inches long, with sharp-pointed, straight, and double blades great for trimming goat hooves.

Jeffers Foot Rot Shears with Serrated Edge – For around $9, these trimmers are designed with one plain side and one with serrated teeth for easy cutting.

Sydell PR Hoof Trimmer – This costs around $16 and is a nice, lightweight trimmer with sharp blades. This particular trimmer is designed for people with small hands.

Biting, Butting, Horning

Sometimes, a goat will decide that it enjoys biting, butting, or horning people. Obviously, these behaviors are not acceptable and must be corrected. Typically, the goat will act in this way as a means of showing dominance. Again, you must teach the goat that you are the boss so the situation does not get out of control. We have provided you with some tips taken from top goat breeders and trainers.

To begin, stand next to the goat. Then, reach down under the belly, grabbing the two legs on the other side of the body. Pull the legs toward you while pushing the goat over using your shoulder. After the goat has fallen to the ground, step over it, taking care to avoid its moving legs.

While doing this, you want to keep holding the front leg while holding the goat's neck down with your hand or knee. By doing this, the goat will not be able to get up.

While this might sound mean, it does not hurt the goat at all. This action quickly shows the goat that you have dominance over it and not the other way around. As you do this, the goat is going to fight and bawl as if you were killing it but you can be sure it is not feeling any pain other than its broken pride.

Continue holding the goat down and eventually, it will quiet down. At that point, you can pet and love it, speaking calmly and softly as you provide reassurance. When you feel the goat has submitted to you, let go so the goat can rise. If the goat moves from you without posturing or turning sideways and hunching its back while tipping its head to the side, then you know your dominance role has been accepted.

On the other hand, if the goat shows posturing, then you will need to repeat this process immediately. The goal is to get the aggressive behavior to stop right then and it very well may. When going through the process again, if the goat should appear to be challenging you – NEVER back up.

The nice aspect of this exercise is that once the goat gets the picture, you can begin offering treats for a few weeks to reinforce the new rules. Your goat needs to understand that you are still a loving, friendly owner but one that can be firm when necessary. If you notice your goat behaving aggressively toward another family member or friend, instruct him or her on how to roll the goat so the behavior with him or her will stop as well.

Catching a Goat

Unless you have raised your goat from a kid, chances are once it is in the pasture it will be difficult to catch. When raised as a baby, many goats will learn their name and actually come when called. Sometimes you can coax the goat in with special treats but most often, the goat will stay put, making the catch challenging.

The first step is to determine why the goat is ignoring you. It might be that the goat is new to your clan, perhaps it is not feeling well, there could be strangers around, or it might simply be that the goat is showing independence. If the goat is new or there are strangers around, you can try the raisins in the hand to see if you can draw the goat in.

If you can get close enough, try scratching the goat's belly or by the ears to calm it down. Usually, if you stand up and begin walking back to the stall, the goat will follow. However, if the goat still refuses to come, try what is referred to as the "following technique."

With this method, you would start by putting the goat in a smaller area, just large enough so it can run around and not get too far from you. Force the goat to run away from you by hollering, as you wave your arms around. In the majority of cases, the goat will run around the far perimeters of the area, allowing you to stay in the center.

From there, walk around in a small circle, making the goat move so it stays ahead of you. However, as the goat begins to run around the outside of the area, the goal is to keep it moving, never stopping. Soon, the goat will become fatigued, wishing it could stop. Your job is to keep hollering and waving your hands to keep the goat moving until it finally starts to breathe hard through its mouth.

By keeping the goat moving, you are teaching it that you have the upper hand. Now, as the goat becomes tired and wants to stop, have the goat turn and go the other direction. If the goat stops all the sudden, very quietly speak to it, offering encouragement to come to you or stand still. Then, begin to walk toward the goat slowly while continuing to talk in a soothing voice. If the goat turns away from you, holler and wave your arms to make it run again.

Keep going with this process until the goat is finally willing to stand still or walk toward you. When you and the goat do meet, stroke it lovingly, petting it for several minutes. You will be amazed at how eager the goat is to please you just to stop running. Once the goat realizes that all you want is for it to stand still, it will comply. This method has been used for years by top trainers, working 99% of the time.

Supplies

When owning a goat, certain tools and supplies should be kept on hand. Although not all of these items will be used daily, they are handy to have around when you do them.

Thermometer – Goats should have a rectal temperature between 101.5 and 103.5 degrees. If you notice that your goat is acting ill, you can take its temperature to get a better idea if it is running a fever.

Dewormers – Using the list of **dewormers** provided or working with your veterinarian, you should keep the appropriate medications on hand.

Hoof Trimmers – Although there are many different types on the market, we recommend the ones listed above.

Furall Spray – If your goat suffers from scrapes or cuts, this spray covers the wound to protect it from dirt. The spray dries quickly, sticking to the wound without hurting the goat.

Probias – To ensure the goat's rumen functions properly, you can use this for illness and stress.

Lice/Mite Dust – During the spring months, goats will sometimes suffer from lice and/or mites. While there are many great products on the market, one that is very affordable and easy to find is called Seven Dust.

Vaccinations, Antibiotics, and Syringes – If you want to administer vaccinations and other medications to your goat, you can maintain both medication and syringes.

Pepto Bismol – On occasion, a goat will get diarrhea. The simplest and most effective treatment is Pepto Bismol.

Tips For Your First Goat

The information above should be very helpful in getting started with your first goat. However, we have gone one-step further by putting together some specific tips that will make the selection process easier.

Wether – A wether is a neutered male that would make a great companion. This goat is good at clearing brush and if you are not interested in milk production a great choice. Wethers maintain a child-like behavior throughout life, are very loving and affectionate, and less expensive to buy then a doe or buck.

Doe – A doe is a female goat that also makes a great companion although she will be in and out of her heat cycle frequently. If you want a goat for breeding and for milk, then you would choose a doe.

Buck – A buck is a male goat that has not been neutered. IMPORANT – you NEVER want a buck. This type of goat does not make a good pet. A buck is used for one thing – breeding. If you want to breed, make sure you have separate living quarters for the buck and always expect him to be a challenge.

Goats do not like being alone, which is why we recommend two, three, or more.

Never buy a goat with horns, even if the animal appears friendly. With horns, there is always risk of injury from being stuck or injury to the animal from becoming caught on something.

Be prepared to care for the goat from the time you buy it through its expected life. In other words, while a kid is cute, it will grow into an adult. Therefore, you need to be committed to the life of the goat – big or small.

Never buy your goat from an auction barn. Here, people usually take their problem goats as a way of getting rid of them. That means while you think you are getting a great goat at an incredible price, you are probably getting a goat that is sick or has serious behavioral problems. Sadly, many of the kids you find at auction barns have been yanked from their mothers before being weaned. These babies often have both emotional and physical problems.

Always buy from a reputable goat breeder known for producing healthy, happy stock. At the end of the "breeding" chapter is a list of some of the breeders we would recommend you consider.

If buying a goat for milking, make sure she has a healthy and well-attached udder, and that she is registered from quality milk stock.

Goats can easily be maintained on one acre or less of land as long as they have adequate access to browse plants (trees and shrubs).

Instead of buying the first goat you see, visit several herds so you have multiple options.

Before you buy a milk goat, ask to taste its milk.

Take time to visit local club meetings, goat shows, or the ADGA so you can meet with professional breeders. This way, you will have the opportunity to ask all the questions you have that were not covered in this book.

Be sure any fencing to the pasture has been made dog-proof and any **poisonous plants** from the list provided removed.

Make sure any dairy goats that you are interested in have been disbudded.

Have the housing for your goat prepared to include a comfortable and safe shelter that is well ventilated and free from drafts. Additionally, the goat will need an outside area where it can run about freely.

Request a copy of the **Caseous Lymphadenitis** and CAE testing results prior to buying the goat.

Follow up with your own veterinarian to see what vaccinations, medications, or dewormers are required for your new goat.

Only buy the best hay for your goat, choosing formulas recommended for the type of goat you have. For example, if you have a dairy goat, then you want to choose a formula of grain designed especially for dairy goats.

Have some type of system in place to keep flies off the goats during the hot summer months.

Keep all food for the goat in a container that is rodent-proof.

Keep powdered minerals and baking soda for your goat on a free-choice basis.

Make sure you have a good veterinarian, one that knows about goats. If you do not have a vet and are not sure where to start looking, you can call around locally or contact reputable goat breeders in your area, asking for references. If all else fails, you can call 1-800-GET-A-DVM.

On average, expect to pay between $3.00 and $4.00 a week to maintain a goat.

Goat popularity is increasing, as more and more people become aware of their many uses.

Before investing in a goat, check with your local city, county, or home association to ensure you can have a goat. Some cities such as Los Angeles in California do not allow farm animals within the city limits. However, if you were to go to Albany, California, you could keep one goat per 150 square feet but just for 60 days as a means of weed control. Therefore, always check local ordinances.

If the goat needs to be socialized from being neglected or simply ignored, you will need to spend adequate time working with the animal to win its trust. In most cases, rescue or abused goats can be rehabilitated but they require additional patience and love. Keep in mind that animal shelters and rescue organizations are very important when taking on a rescued goat, often having special programs for this effort.

If you already have a goat with horns or have fallen in love with a goat that has horns one of three things should happen. First, do not buy the goat. Second, you could talk to your veterinarian about having the horns surgically removed. The problem is that this option is expensive and if the goat is full grown, it could be harmful. Third, work with the goat through training and tons of patience. If you choose to keep the horns, remember that you always need to be aware of your surroundings whenever out with the goat. Simple play could cause an accidental stick that could be deadly.

Proper Food and Housing

In this chapter, we will discuss the appropriate food and housing required for goats. Goats in their natural environment will roam about freely, eating large quantities of browse as they go. With fast metabolisms, they are constantly eating, stopping to rest on occasion.

Food Tips

One of the misconceptions about goats is that they will eat the weeds out of a person's yard. While they may, you cannot purchase a goat expecting that it will simply pick out the weeds and leave your perfectly manicured lawn alone.

A goat has a digestive system very much like a sheep or cow, meaning they are grazers that love grass. However, goats are actually more as deer when it comes to food, both being considered browsers. This means if the goat had its choice, it would stick with trees and brush over grass.

For that reason, if you want a goat to clean up your property, you have probably chosen the wrong animal. In fact, chances are the goat would walk right past the weeds, eager to reach your prized rose bushes. Therefore, it is important that you buy a goat for the right reasons.

Goats have a very high nutritional need. When they have a deficiency, health problems arise. With goats, the requirement for food varies with growth, production, and the type of production system. Excluding the dairy goats, this animal needs high quality browse and forage because of its nutritional value.

In fact, goats will eat as much as five pounds of dry matter per 100 pounds of body weight every day! In addition, the stages of the goat's maturity along with how this growth affects the forage quality are also a consideration. It boils down to knowing how to match the goat's nutrient needs to the forage quality.

Once you understand this, you can save money by not having to buy as much supplemental grain. Now, there are times when supplement grain is imperative. For example, if browse and forage were not available on your land, during the cold winter months, or during dry spells, then grain or hay would need to be added to the goat's diet.

Goats need a lot of roughage to survive. For this reason, they need to have plenty of opportunity to eat dry forage and hay. You would think this roughage would be hard on their stomachs but remember goats have a four-chamber stomach that can process this type of food with no problem. In addition, a goat's food is digested with live bacteria found in hay.

Goats should never be fed grain and grain products only because it is simply too hard for them to digest. In this case, any food remaining undigested would be eliminated from the goat's body as urine or feces. With this, Urinary Calculi, Founder, Hypocalcemia, and other similar problems could occur. The same is true in providing your goat with wrong levels of minerals, vitamins, and nitrogen.

While we see cattle and other red meats that marble, a goat's meat does not do that. Instead, the layers of fat lying around the kidneys, liver, and heart impair optimum function. Therefore, if the goat is fed a continual diet of grain, serious health problems will occur and the bones of the goat will not grow strong enough to hold the body's weight.

For any goat, whether a kid or adult, creep feeding of grains is the best option. This means the goats would be permitted to roam about at will, devouring the various types of browse offered. If you want to offer your goat grain, you can but make sure you provide it in very small quantities. In addition, any grain not consumed by the goat in 15 minutes should be taken away.

When looking for the best goat feed, start by considering your soil. This is important since the soil will serve as the foundation for the amounts of minerals and vitamins being consumed. You should also have your hay tested to determine its nutrient content. With this information, you could work with a good nutritionist in creating the perfect feed for your beloved goats.

A nice mix of food for your goat would include clover, grass, and alfalfa. This offers the goat a balanced diet that meets all its nutritional needs. You can also add a small amount of pellet grain if you like but make sure you choose only that intended for goats. Some goats like sweet food so a blend such as Nutrina is a great choice that goats love.

For some bucks and neutered male goats, the amount of grain offered should be limited. The reason is that too much grain can cause a condition known as **urinary calculi**, as mentioned earlier in the book. This buildup of small crystals or stones in the goat's bladder is extremely painful and if not treated immediately, it can kill. Therefore, to avoid the possibility of this occurring, simply keep the grain away from the males. Remember, if you want to add a small amount of grain you can but it is crucial that you choose grain that consists of ammonium chloride.

To keep the goat's food clean and uncontaminated, a hayrack is a great investment. This way, the hay and grain will not be sitting on the floor along with the urine and feces. Instead, the goat's food is off the ground in a controlled and clean container. The same is true for the water supply. Goats need fresh water daily, again kept in a container that is up off the floor.

As you prepare to buy food for your goat, remember the two most important vitamins are A and D. Vitamin A keeps the lining of the goat's body, both inside and outside, healthy. When goats are young, Vitamin A is needed in larger quantity, which can be provided through green leafy hay. Another great source that goats love is yellow corn, which contains carotene. If the corn has yellow pigmentation, this is converted into Vitamin A by the goat.

Vitamin D is also required by the goat. With this, proper use of phosphorous and calcium occurs to help build strong bones. Interestingly, sun on the goat's skin can actually convert steroids into Vitamin D. For this reason, goats need to get several hours of sun each day. You can also benefit from hay that has been cured in the sun. If you have concern about your goat getting adequate amounts of Vitamin D, you can add irradiated yeast to the grain. Just be sure to follow the instructions carefully since too much can be harmful.

Other important minerals include phosphorous and calcium along with iodine and selenium, in some areas. If your goat is eating grain and alfalfa hay, chances are its phosphorous and calcium needs are being met. However, if the goat is eating only from a pasture, then consider adding a mineral mixture of equal parts to include steamed bone meal, iodized salt, and limestone. Remember, a lactating doe and young kids have high needs of these minerals so make sure the levels are being met.

Just as vitamins must be given in the right amount, both phosphorous and calcium must also be given in the right quantity. If the goat is given too much, harm can be done. As hinted to, some regions have a **deficiency of iodine and selenium**. Although rare, it can happen. If this were the case, then you would find muscle disease affecting the goat. Keep in mind that when treating goats with minerals, you must be careful in that these toxic substances. The best option is to work closely with your veterinarian to determine the appropriate amount.

Poisonous Plants

As mentioned briefly, some plants are very dangerous to goats. To make sure you avoid these, we have listed the exact things you need to keep out of your goat's reach.

Almond (seeds only)

Amanita Mushrooms (all parts)

American Bittersweet (berries, roots, and leaves)

Apple (large amount of seeds only)

Apricot (seeds only)

Autumn Crocus (all parts excluding the bulb)

Avocado (leaves only)

Azalea (all parts)

Black-Eyed Susan (all parts)

Black Locust (bark, twigs, and seeds)

Bleeding Heart (leaves and roots)

Boxwood (leaves and twigs)

Buckeye (leaves, nuts, flowers, and sprouts)

Buttercup (all parts)

Caladium (all parts)

Castor Bean (both seeds and leaves)

Chinaberry (fruit, bark, and berries)

Christmas Rose (root, leaves, and sap)

Chokecherry (leaves, seeds, and bark)

Cone Flower (all parts)

Daffodil (all parts)

Daphne (all parts)

Deadly Nightshade (all parts)

Diffenbachia (all parts)

Dutchman's Breeches (leaves and roots)

English Holly (berries only)

English Ivy (berries and leaves)

Foxglove (leaves only)

Golden Chain (seeds, pods, and flowers)

Hemlock (seeds, stems, and fleshy taproot)

Horsechestnut (all parts)

Iris (corms)

Jack in the Pulpit (all parts)

Jonquil (all parts)

Jumson Weed (all parts)

Lantana (green berries and leaves)

Larkspur (all parts including the seeds)

Lily of the Valley (all parts)

Mistletoe (berries only)

Monkshood (all parts)

Morning Glory (seeds only)

Mountain Laurel (all parts including honey from flowers)

Narcissus (all parts)

Nightshade (all parts)

Oak (tannins in foliage and acorns)

Oleander (all parts)

Philodendron (all parts)

Pokeweed (roots, shoots, and leaves)

Potatoes (all green parts)

Privet (leaves and berries)

Rhodendendron (all parts)

Rhubarb (leaves only)

Rosary Pea (seeds only)

Tobacco (leaves only)

Tomatoes (leaves only)

Tulip (bulbs only)

Velvet Grass (all parts)

White Snakeroot (all parts)

Wild Black Cherry (all parts)

Wisteria (pods and seeds)

Yellow Jasmine (all parts including the nectar and roots)

Yew (all parts excluding berries)

Housing Tips

In addition to providing your goat with a clean stall, it will also need a place where it can get out of the elements and where it will be warm and dry. Because goats do not do well when cooped up, they must have room to roam where they can browse at will. Confining your goats to small pastures or stalls will actually increase their exposure to worms. To help reduce the problem with parasites, always perform pasture rotation.

For goat ranching, try to have a minimum of four pastures that can be used on rotation for the goats. Typically, you would place the goats in one pasture for about two months and then move them around. This will allow the browse to grow and keep the parasite problem down. If you have a pasture with other goats or animals, allow the goats to graze.

The bigger concern is regarding dangerous plants that the goat may get into. If you have cattle that graze, you can usually keep anywhere from one to three goats for every cow, as long as there is adequate food for all.

For the pasture, you need to have the right type of fence. For goats, the best choice is a woven wire fence but remember, if your goats have horns, this type of fence creates the prime opportunity for the goat to become caught. Another option that works well is a high tensile electric fence made with five strands. This type of fence is not overly expensive and very easy to maintain.

Now, as far as housing for your goats, this will depend on the production system you prefer. In other words, if you plan to keep brush or fiber control, and plan raising meat goats, housing will provide protection for the goats from rain, snow, and wind. With this, a standard type barn or rock outcropping would work well.

On the other hand, if you plan to raise dairy goats, you want a building where the goats can be milked. This way, any kids can be kept near the mother while protecting both doe and kid from harsh elements.

For the bedding, the best option is dry, clean straw although pine shavings also work well. To keep the odor level down, sprinkle lime underneath the bedding to help absorption of the urine and feces moisture. Finally, make sure when the goats are outside, they have blocks of wood, barrels, cement, and other items on which to climb. Goats of all breeds love to climb, needing toys for play.

Fence Construction

Putting up a fence for goats provides needed protection and safety. Although the cost of the fence will depend on the type chosen, the location of your fence is the most important factor, especially since not all fences work in the same type area.

Electric

Electric fences have been used for generations. This type of fence can be set up as a temporary or permanent solution, using a ground wire running about every four strands of hot wires. With an electric fence, should the goat try to jump or push through, it would be given a safe jolt of electricity.

Field

The field fence is the most expensive although once constructed, the cost of maintenance is very little. This fence measures 32 inches tall, with 12 inch spacing between the vertical stays.

Then, there are two strands of barbed, electric, or smooth wire added to the top for height. If you live in a region where it snows and decide to go with a field fence, you may be required to add wooden stays for support due to the weight of the snow.

Modified Cattle

With this option, you would have a three or four-strand barbwire fence converted for housing goats. All you need to do is add an electric wire below and between the existing strands. Then, the strands are mounted to wooden posts. This method is very economical since you can simply modify an existing fence.

Sheep

The sheep fence is easy to put up around specific areas. However, this type of fence is not a good deterrent for goats with horns who have decided the grass is greener on the other side. While the design of the fence can vary, you would generally see four of six-inch squares that are close together to keep the goats from escaping or pushing through.

Goats and Their Wool

In addition to breeding goats for meat, dairy, and family pets, goats also have another purpose – wool! Funny thing is that most people think of wool coming only from sheep but in fact, several soft and lustrous fibers come from the goat.

Hair

With goats, there are three specific types of hair. Keep in mind that one type of hair is not necessarily better than another type, simply different with unique characteristics.

Type A - Angora

This first type of goat hair is very long and lustrous. The fibers measure six inches on average, falling into curly locks. With this type of coat, it is not always obvious on the "Type A" animal. Fibers are like fine mohair and gorgeous. Some of these goats are single coated and therefore, must be shorn, which would include the Pygoras.

Type B - Blend

With the blend type of goat hair, the goat has an under-coat, which is a wonderful blend of Angora mohair and cashmere. Typically, the strands of fiber measure between three and six inches in length and feature a soft crimp or curl. In many cases, this second coat cannot be seen.

Keep in mind that with the blend goat hair, the fleece can have a matte, dull finish, or a shiny, lustrous finish. Of all goat hair types, Type B Blend is the most common, which must be shorn, plucked, or combed.

Type C - Cashmere

The fibers from this type of goat hair are very fine and without luster. The length generally ranges from one to three inches. The hair appears almost coarse, especially when compared with Type A and Type B. Cashmere sweaters and other apparel items you see sold today are made from this type of hair. With cashmere, the hair must be shorn or combed.

Angora

The Angora goat is what produces beautiful mohair. Since this particular breed of goat is not good for meat because of the small body frame and low production of kids, people use the fibers instead.

In most cases, Angoras are bred in the state of Texas. With the mohair, you will find beautiful and ultra soft sweaters, jackets, and a number of other apparel items. In addition, mohair is commonly used for yarn, worked to create scarves, sweaters, coats, and any type of crocheting and knitting project.

Cashmere

A Cashmere goat is actually a cross breed. The undercoat of the Cashmere goat produces the magnificent cashmere sweaters, coats, and other items that people pay a hefty price for owning. Cashmere apparel is luxurious and considered a real luxury to own.

Interestingly, some Cashmere goats produce such large quantities of cashmere that they are shorn at the end of the winter season in addition to normal shearing times. For cashmere taken from the goat to be usable, the fleece must be kept clean all year long. Although this requires a little more time and effort, the result is perfect fleece that produces top quality cashmere, which turns a pretty penny for the goat rancher.

Milking a Goat

A common reason for owning goats is for the milk and milk by-products that can be produced. As you can imagine, people getting started with dairy goats have tons of questions. In this chapter, we will address some of the factors associated with milking a goat that are of the highest interest.

Dairy Goats

Remember that when buying a dairy goat, not all females will product milk. As discussed in an earlier chapter, **dairy goats** would include any of the following:

Alpine – 3.5% butterfat

Broken

Chamoise/Chamoisee

Cou Blanc

Cou Clair

Cou Noir

Pied

Sundgau

Two-Tone Chamoise/Chamoisee

LaMancha – 4.2% butterfat

Nigerian Dwarf – 6.1% butterfat

Nubian – 4.6% butterfat

Oberhasli – 3.6% butterfat

Saanen – 3.5% butterfat

Toggenburg – 3.3% butterfat

Milk Production

When owning female goats that do produce milk, you should understand the natural cycle associated with milking, which will help you determine how much milk you will get. When a goat gives birth to kids, also called freshening, she will begin to produce milk, known as lactating. Typically, the amount of milk produced at first will be slight but then over time, it will increase primarily because of supply and demand from the kids.

As her babies begin to grow and experiment with grasses and grains, the amount of nursing will decrease, thus the amount of milk produced also decreases. During this time, the doe will begin to wean the babies so that eventually (usually by three months) she will be done nursing and the lactating will stop.

After the goat's milk has dried up, she will eventually go into her heat cycle again at which time she would be bred. Once she becomes pregnant and gives birth, the milk production cycle starts over. If you allow the cycle to takes its natural course and if she is milked twice a day by you, she would dry out sooner.

Remember, if you do milk your goat, you need to give her a minimum of two months before being bred again. In fact, many top goat breeders give the doe up to five months off! Keep in mind that certain things can be done to help a doe produce large quantities of milk. First, she would need to be milked every day so there is a constant demand for milk. This stimulates the continuing production of milk. Second, she must be kept on a high grain diet to keep nutrients up so she can produce both quantity and quality of milk.

Remember, the production of milk will decrease as the doe goes through the lactation process whether nursing a kid or being milked by a human. That means that even with consistent milking and a high grain diet, she will eventually dry up no matter what you do. This is completely normal and part of the lactating process.

Your best option is to keep a journal of the amount of milk your doe is producing. With this, you can tell when the milk production is starting to decrease. In addition, the journal will help you watch for any potential health risks during this process. Although you can come up with your own system, most people prefer to track by weight instead of milk volume. With that, you know the exact amount of milk. If you count volume, you would also be counting the heavy butterfat and protein, which gives you a false reading.

Instead, use a normal water equivalent of eight pounds to one gallon. With a standard hanging scale, weigh the bucket and then after milking the goat, deduct the total weight minus the bucket weight to come up with the actual milk weight. It is important to maintain a record for each goat since different breeds produce different weight milk and milk production varies from one breed to another.

In addition to tracking the weight of the milk, keep track of the date and time of day when the goat is milked. In addition, if you notice any problems on a particular day, mark that down as well. With that information, you can determine on a weekly or monthly basis how much milk your little girl is producing for you.

Choosing a Dairy Goat

When you are ready to buy a dairy goat, you will discover they are shown by age, breed, and gender. Many times, the kids one year or younger will be separated down into several classes based on the date of their birth. If the kid is older but has not yet given birth, then it would be considered a "dry yearling", which goes up to two years of age.

For a doe less than two years that has had kids, she would be shown as "milking yearlings." Remember, to be considered fully mature, the dairy goat would need to be three to four years old. Now, if the doe were more than five years of age, she would be labeled as an "aged doe", meaning she shows in her own class.

Milking Process

To milk a goat, put the doe on the milk stand so her teats are at the right level for milking. Then, after tethering her, offer her some grain or raisins to keep her calm and stress free. One recommendation - if your doe has gone through kidding, it would be better to wait two weeks before milking. The reason is that the milk right after giving birth tends to have a strange taste caused by the high level of colostrum and hormones. While it will not hurt you, most people do not like the taste.

When milking your doe for the first time, start by shaving around the udder to keep the milk clean. This will also make the milking process easier so you do not have to work around hair.

Then, take a teat in each hand and while holding firmly, pull down and squeeze. For milk to be expressed, you do not have to be rough, just a consistent motion. With a little practice, you will be able to milk your goat in no time.

In addition to the actual milk, goat milk makes delicious cheese. In fact, if you were to visit any number of five-star restaurants, you would see goat cheese offered on the menu. Because goat's milk has a little different composition than you would see with cow's milk, it might take a little getting used to.

However, while some people have to acquire a taste for goat's milk and by-products, many people love it the first time they taste it. Goat's milk is excellent for people who are lactose intolerant. In fact, most can handle this type of milk with no problem.

Dairy Operation

Some people get so involved with dairy goats that they start a small coop to sell the milk and milk by-products. If your goal is to own dairy goats for mass production of milk, you will need to consider several important aspects.

Some factors include hiring enough labor, marketing your product, processing the milk, understanding and following governmental regulations, staying within a budget, following strict economics, and so on. Just to give you a few suggestions, consider the labor and marketing aspects of this endeavor.

Labor

For some people, they will begin the dairy coop as a family business that involves little to no outside help. While this is fine when getting started, you need a good idea of your goals, realizing that your business could grow quickly. With that, you would need to hire additional labor to keep up with customer demand.

Remember, caring for and milking goats is big business that requires long, hard hours of work. Other people following this same dream will tell you they love it but that they work 365 days a year – no holidays off. In addition to the milking, there are stalls to clean, food to prepare, shots and vaccinations to give, deworming and disbudding to perform, and all the things that go along with keeping dairy goats.

The required labor will vary but it is estimated that a dairy coop with 100 dairy goats selling fluid milk to a processor will take 1.5 full-time people. Consider the time involved on a daily basis for this type of operation. You have the milking, set up and clean up, manure handling and bedding, heat detection, feeding grain and hay, breeding, and the list goes on.

Obviously for labor alone, the number of hours invested would depend on the number of dairy goats. Therefore, if you are serious about milking dairy goats, keep in mind that you have the investment of both money and time. This business is serious and to get and keep customers, you need to maintain a clean and efficient facility. To do that, you need adequate labor.

Marketing

Before marketing can be established, customers need to know what you have to offer them. However, it is your job to determine what you want to offer. Some people sell only fluid milk while other people with a milking goat coop will sell cream, butter, cheese, and so on. To make this decision, crunch numbers to make sure a profit can be made and if so, on which products.

For selling fluid goat milk, a reputable and reliable buyer will need to be identified. Many people have invested their life savings to start a coop but because they failed to set up buyers, they went out of business in less than one year. To ensure this does not happen to you, educate yourself on selling goat milk and goat milk products.

In addition, have your shipping organized, packaging chosen, pricing set, and everything in order so that your next step is to get the word out to everyone possible that you have something great to offer. Remember that marketing requires payment upfront but if done right, it can take a small family-owned dairy coop, turning it into a very successful business.

Meat Operation

As you know, some people get involved with the meat aspect of goats, which may or may not also include hides. Just as with dairy, this is a huge undertaking but if done right, it too can be very lucrative.

For starters, you need to know everything possible, not just about meat goats but about the operation and all it takes to get the business started. This means learning things such as demand so you know how to meet the customer's needs. As an example, Cabrito or Chevron as it is sometimes called (goat meat) has such a high demand in the United States alone that people who are raising goats for meat cannot keep up.

Because of this, much of the goat meat found in the United States comes from other countries such as Australia and New Zealand. In fact, this is such a serious business that approximately 1.5 million pounds of goat meat is imported to the United States each week. The good news is that demand is rising. For meat growers, this is money in the bank and job security.

If you wonder why such a high demand, much of this is because of changing ethnic demographics of the continent. This swing is so dramatic that today, 63% of all red meat consumed around the globe is goat meat. What we see in the United States is a growing population of Asian, African, Latin American, Middle Eastern, and the Caribbean heritages, which has boosted goat meat sales.

Goat meat is actually easy on the stomach and with so many people suffering from some type of digestive problem, an easy diet. The reason is that goat meat has a different molecular structure from other forms of meat, especially red meat, meaning it can be digested far better. In addition, not only is goat meat low fat but it is actually very tasty. The type of goat the meat comes from makes a difference in taste, which is why most people prefer at least 75% Boer.

For some reason, Boer makes the meat milder, which is often compared to veal. Therefore, when thinking about going into business with goat meat, learn about the various tastes produced by the different breeds as well as the type of goat meat the public prefers.

Niche

As you begin searching for your market niche, you definitely want to consider direct marketing. This type of buyer or group of buyers will come to your ranch or farm, buying the goats from you. Typically, direct marketing groups are associated with ethnic restaurants, FFA clubs, 4-H groups, and so on.

If you live in an area near numerous ethnic restaurants, this would be an excellent option for marketing. In addition to local restaurants, you might also reach out to meat breeding stock. While you might make $1.00 per pound from most groups, many times, commercial meat breeders will offer double that or more for breeding stock.

Team Work

In the goat meat industry, many smaller coops work together. In other words, if you were interested in starting a family business, you might find other meat coops operated by families in the same area. Rather than become competitors, set something up to piggyback off each other's business. With this, you could supply goat meat to markets all across the country because now, you have more goats and thus, more meat.

Slaughterhouses

Whatever you do, avoid being sucked into thinking a slaughterhouse is a reputable meat business. With slaughterhouses, the meat is often poor quality and in many cases, not even meat type goats. For this reason, you want to run a quality operation that runs with integrity. That means raising healthy meat goats and processing them in a humane, effective manner.

Auction Houses

While you might be tempted to buy goats from an auction house, we strongly discourage this. In most cases, auctions are better for selling goats than for buying them. The reason is that the percentage of healthy goats from an auction house is low. Remember, if you are going to start your business, you want the best even if you have to pay a little more.

Herd Sire and Full Blood

You will need to determine if you are willing to make an upfront investment to start a herd of quality breeders. If you look at all the industries associated with livestock, you would see that there is always room for quality, registered herd sire. However, understand these goats would have to be fertile, disease free, adaptable, prolific, and have muscle and meat consistency that would deem them commercial quality.

The bottom line is that if you begin only with a meat herd but add in a full blood sire, you will at some point need to consider buying a full blood doe so the sire will have someone for breeding. With this comes another decision of producing herd sires for all the local people and not necessarily for businesses.

In reality, this idea is a good one because the sale of just one full blood one time a year will pay about one-fifth of the feed for 50 other goats being raised. With goat meat, it is all about good business. This involves knowing all you can about the various breeds, understanding how you need to create your herd, what feed they need to be on, and so on.

With a goat meat business, the complications are greater than you would face with a dairy coop. Pricing can be a little more challenging and the market is very different. However, if you have a genuine interest of raising meat goats and breaking into the business, you can and do quite well.

The fascinating aspect of this is that meat goats are both the newest and fastest growing small acreage opportunity in the entire country. Just remember that making the purchase of meat goats should never be made on a whim – this requires precision planning and in-depth research.

Getting Started

As mentioned, Boers are considered among the best for meat. However, other types of goats can be raised for meat to include Kiko, Tennessee Fainting, and Spanish breeds.

Keep in mind that just three of these are considered true breeds for meat by the various breed associations, which would include the Boer, Kiko, and Tennessee Fainting goats. Although the Spanish goat has proven to be great for breeding, currently there is no breeding standards or registry at this time.

When looking over your options of the breed that you want to consider, also consider bringing in a few top quality full bloods to your operation since they are beneficial. With this, if you find your business skyrockets and demand explodes, the demand for the full blood goats will also increase and you will be covered all the way around.

If you were unsure where to start, we would recommend you contact reputable goat breeders in your area, especially those that raise meat goats. Schedule time with as many of these breeders as you can, meeting with them to learn everything imaginable. Look for a breeder from which you can buy goats.

Make sure the goats are registered and tattooed. For your own protection, check the tattoo with the registration papers to make sure they match. You also want to walk around the breeding farm, checking stalls, arenas, and all around for cleanliness and organization.

Ask about the birthing history of the goats interested in buying to ensure you buy goats with a history of easy and healthy births. In addition, question if there have been any problems with the doe and/or buck, types of vaccinations, dewormers, and other medications used, etc. No matter where you buy your goats, always ask yourself the following questions:

Will the goat meet your needs?

Do the farms you are looking at use their goats for the same purpose as you will?

Are you impressed with the farm and the overall operation relating to its cleanliness, structure, schedule, appearance, and so on?

Are the goats in sound health and have they been raised in a comfortable and safe environment?

When looking at breeding stock, does the selling price include future breeding or semen?

Will the goats be sold with health certificates and if not, will the seller pay for them?

Is the seller of the goats knowledgeable about goats and the farming operation?

Summary

We are at the conclusion of the book and sincerely hope that you have learned enough about goats to make educated decisions. Goats are truly amazing animals. They are extremely versatile creatures, which is why so many people are both amazed and fascinated by them. Unlike some other animals, goats are very smart and very loving.

As you learned, the reason for purchasing and raising goats varies. Whether looking for a goat for milk, meat, or a family pet, we are confident this book has provided you with great insight into the world of goats. We also believe that with the information read, you will make the right choices. Obviously, there are many other aspects to owning goats but we have done our best to answer some of the most commonly asked questions and then some.

to any specific commercial products, process, or service by trade name, trademark, manufacturer, or otherwise, does not necessarily constitute or imply its endorsement, recommendation, or favoring.

We thank you for allowing us to open the doors to the world of goats and we wish you much success regardless of your endeavor.

Resources

Although there are far too many resources to ever name, we have put together some that we believe you will find useful. These resources along with the ones you will discover on your own will get you on your way to being the best goat owner around!

Top Breeders

We have identified some of what we considered the top breeders of goats. Whether you buy from these or simply gain information from their experience, we believe this will get you started in the right direction.

CAGBA (Colored Angora Goat Breeding Association –

http://www.cagba.org – Founded in 1998, this organization is the registry and representing body for the Colored Angora Goats in both the United States and Canada.

Boer Goat Breeder's Association of Australia –

http://boergoat.une.edu.au – With more than 770 members, this association is the sole register for Boer goats in Australia.

Internet Farm Index –

http://www.ifi-us.com/goats.asp - This online resource is a wealth of information. Owned by Botany Zone Incorporated, you will find tons of farms and breeders associated with goats. Every breed, farming needs, equipment, supplies – you name it, information is available here.

Cybergoat –

http://www.cybergoat.com/links/meat_goat.shtml   - This website is loaded with name after name of top breeder for all types of goats.

MAC Goats –

http://members.psyber.com/macgoats - Just moved to the Ozarks in Missouri, these breeders have some of the finest!

Goatweb Breeder's Directory –

http://www.goatweb.com/breeders_directory/index.sht ml - This site is loaded with tons of breeders around the country, making it an excellent resource!

MAX Boer Goats –

http://www.maxboergoats.com – Top breeding Boer goats from this farm in Pennsylvania.

Ranch & Rural Directory –

http://www.ranchmagazine.com/breeder.html - Here you will find excellent breeder information for all breeds of goats.

Online Supplies

Again, there are thousands and thousands of businesses selling supplies for goat owners. However, we have pulled some together to help you get started.

Nelson Manufacturing –

http://www.nelsonmfg.com – This Company specializes in both design and manufacturing of all types of farm animal supplies and equipment. Founded in 1949, everything you need and more can be found here.

Premier1Supplies –

http://www.premier1supplies.com – For more than 25 years, Premier1Supplies has been providing all types of goat supplies, fencing, and more.

Caprine Supply –

http://www.caprinesupply.com – With 50 years in the goat supply and equipment business, you will be astounded by the vast selection in their online catalog.

Hoegger Goat Supply –

http://hoeggergoatsupply.com – In business since 1935, Hoegger's understands the goat business!

SpringCreek Goat Supply –

http://www.springcreekgoatsupplies.com – Great products, information, and supplies.